THE COMPLEX FORMS OF THE RELIGIOUS LIFE

American Academy of Religion
Academy Series
Edited by
Carl A. Raschke

Frances Westley

THE COMPLEX FORMS
OF THE RELIGIOUS LIFE
A Durkheimian View
of New Religious Movements

Scholars Press
Chico, California

THE COMPLEX FORMS OF THE RELIGIOUS LIFE
A Durkheimian View of New Religious Movements

by
Frances Westley
Ph.D., 1978, McGill University
Montreal, Quebec

© 1983
American Academy of Religion

Library of Congress Cataloging in Publication Data

Westley, Frances.
  The complex forms of the religious life.

  (American Academy of Religion academy series ; no.
45)
    Bibliography: p.
    1. Religion and sociology—History—20th Century.
2. Cults—History—20th century. 3. Durkheim, Émile,
1858–1917. I. Title. II. Series.
BL60.W47   1983   306'.6   83–4579
ISBN 0-89130-626-9

Printed in the United States of America

In the effort of researching and writing this work, I am indebted to a number of people. First and foremost, I am indebted to Michael Carroll, who advised me in its writing and conception and unfailingly provided a clear head and a steadying influence. Secondly, I am indebted to Frederick Bird, who conceived of and headed the Concordia project on new religious movements, and whose ideas and insights were most helpful. I am also indebted to the other members of the Concordia research team, in particular Susan Palmer, whose intriguing thesis on Shakti attracted me to the study of this particular kind of group. I am indebted to the Canada Council and the Quebec government for the doctoral fellowship and research grant which financed my doctoral study and research. I am indebted to Joyce Granich whose typing and editing of the manuscript was an invaluable aid in its completion. Lastly, I am indebted to the members of the groups themselves, without whose cooperation this book could not have been written.

TABLE OF CONTENTS

vii

LIST OF TABLES

SECTION I

RELIGION IN A COMPLEX SOCIETY: DURKHEIM'S
PREDICTIONS AND THE NEW RELIGIOUS MOVEMENTS

In defense of his book Elementary Forms, Durkheim
indicated that the study of very primitive or simple forms
was the first step towards a study of the more "complicated"
modern forms of religious life.

It is because a science in its infancy must pose problems in their simplest form, and only later make them
gradually more complicated. When we have understood
very elementary religions we will be able to move on
to others. (Durkheim, 1919:134-5)

Durkheim's theories, particularly those relating
religious beliefs and rituals to social forms, have been used
extensively by anthropologists and social anthropologists but
have been largely ignored by sociologists. This has been due
to several factors. Durkheim's analysis of Elementary Forms
described a cohesive culture, all members of which participated in an overarching symbol system. Modern society
(particularly contemporary society) presents a picture of
religious and cultural plurality with little consensus about
symbols. It also offers a picture of secularization, of a
situation in which increasing numbers of people do not seem
to participate in any religion.

A closer study of Durkheim suggests, however, that
Durkheim foresaw both the above factors and found them not
incompatible with his basic theories about the relation
between religion and social order. In fact, in other
articles, Durkheim suggested that as society evolved so would
religion, and that in a modern, complex society religion
would reflect the diversity and specialization of that
society. Religion would not die out, however, for men would
always need a symbolic arena for expressing what they still
had in common.

The pun in the title of this dissertation is, therefore,
intentional. What this work hopes to accomplish is an
examination of those forms of modern religion which seem to

capture and express the essence of life in a modern, complex
society, in the way in which the primitive cult explored in
The Elementary Forms of the Religious Life was revealed to
articulate life in a primitive society. To this end we will
follow the general outline of Durkheim's study, focusing in
turn on the relationship between beliefs and social organization, and the function of rituals in a selection of new
religious movements, which we shall term, after Durkheim, the
"cult of man."

CHAPTER I

EMILE DURKHEIM'S SOCIOLOGY OF RELIGION

Emile Durkheim's theories of religion are primarily
developed in his 1913 work, The Elementary Forms of the
Religious Life (although his interest in religion predates
this work). In this book, Durkheim drew a series of con-
clusions about the nature of religion based on ethnographic
data gathered from a primitive Australian tribe, the Arunta.
His purpose was not only to "explain" this "most simple" form
of religious life (as a scientist would examine a most
primitive life form like the amoeba) but to use it as a basis
for making hypotheses about religion in general. As our
concern is with Durkheim's predictions about the future of
religion, it is worth examining those elements which he
postulated as basic to all religions.

In this analysis we have adopted Stephen Lukes'
classification of Durkheim's hypotheses, as it provides an
efficient but complete understanding of the aspects of
Durkheim's thought on religion. Lukes indicates that
Durkheim's hypotheses may be divided into three groups:
causal, representational and functional (Lukes, 1975:462).

His causal theories about religion postulate a structural correspondence between social structure and religious
organization as manifested in beliefs and rituals. The
latter, it is argued, is derived from the former. What will
be held sacred in any social group is what members of that
group hold in common. This theory leads directly to
Durkheim's hypotheses about the representational aspects of
religion.

The representational elements of religion may be seen as
twofold. First, Durkheim felt that religion expresses,
symbolically and metaphorically, the individual's relations
to society and the sentiments engendered by collective life.
Secondly, it serves a cognitive or interpretive function. By
mirroring society, religion allows society to see itself, to
become self-conscious.

3

Durkheim's functional theories about religion form the third group of hypotheses. Religion functions to order life both on an individual (microscopic) and societal (macroscopic) level. In the former instances, Durkheim suggests that the individual's behavior and motivations are regulated by his interactions with the sacred as manifested in collective gatherings. This regulatory process is largely contained in the rites or ritual acts which any religion prescribes for its adherents and which serve to empower the individual (in the case of positive rituals) and restrict the individual (in the case of negative rituals). On the larger, societal level religion serves to order social life by maintaining social order and providing social integration on a moral and/or cultural level.

Criticism has been levelled at Durkheim that as his theories are based on such a restricted (and often faulty) data base, they cannot be generalized to other societies, particularly to our post-industrial and technological age. It is important to remember, however, that Durkheim was an evolutionist. As he posited a relation between social and religious organization, it follows that as social organization evolves so would the content of religious rituals and beliefs. In addition, Durkheim felt that the representational and functional aspects of religion would evolve. Particularly the cognitive, or interpretive role of religion in traditional society was bound to be usurped by the sciences and social sciences as these gathered momentum and interpretive power.

The only immutable aspects of religion, Durkheim argued, were its expressive aspects, and its ability to provide motivation. Man's need to express his relation to society would never vanish: "Symbolic representations are as necessary for the well-working of our moral life as food is for the maintenance of our physical self" (Lukes, 1975:475). Nor would man's need for motivation and the sense of being "empowered" ever be satisfied better than by religious gatherings and rituals. Finally, religious beliefs and rituals would continue to be an expression of what held society together. To the extent that these beliefs were in disarray and religious practices indecisive, society could be seen as in a state of transition (Ibid.:475).

It is this latter point which has come under criticism in Durkheim's time as well as in our own. In a highly technological society, based on utilitarian individualism and increasingly specialized and diversified, how is it possible (it is argued) to expect cultural integration on any basis besides that of the demands of the marketplace?

Durkheim's answer to this was ingenious; at once a defense of individualism and a reiteration that man was a social animal and that this would be nowhere more apparent than in his religion.

Durkheim predicted that as society becomes more differentiated and highly specialized, geographically and culturally diversified, men would come to feel that they had little in common besides their sheer humanity. The resulting cult he suggested would be the "cult of man" -- a cult in which the human individual, idealized, would be worshipped and held sacred.

This idea first emerged in 1897 in the concluding chapter of Suicide. Having established that suicide resulted from an imbalance in the individual's relation to society, as an outcome of over or under-evaluation of individual autonomy, Durkheim stressed that not only a degree of freedom but a degree of restraint was necessary for individual survival. These restraints were best exercised by religion. In a society increasingly dominated by individualism where freedoms for the individual were being daily won, Durkheim suggested that the defense of these individual rights must become the religion in order to hold people together, motivate them as a group and protect the individual from anomie (1951:336-38).

Durkheim resurrected his idea about the "cult of man" in much greater detail the following year in a paper, "Individualism and the Intellectuals" (Durkheim, 1969 tr.). This paper, was meant as a defense of Dreyfus and an attack on those who equated the protection of individual rights with the sacrifice of social order. In it he suggested that increasing individualism, closely linked as it was with differentiation, was the irrepressible wave of the future (Ibid.:26). Not only was it encouraged by "population

growth, geographical expansion and increasing social differentiation," but by our Christian heritage and morality which
transferred "the very centre of the moral life from outside
to within and (set up) the individual as the sovereign judge"
(Ibid.:27). To defend these liberties is therefore to defend
the very fabric of society, that which we must increasingly
rely upon to hold people together. To worship the idealized
individual was not egoistic but raised the individual personality above itself, empowering it as religions have always
done and yet providing social integration through a common
cause.

As in traditional religion, Durkheim predicted that this
"cult of man" would represent and dramatize social relations
on the expressive level. By this he meant that those aspects
which individuals in a society felt that they had in common
would be represented as sacred in the religious beliefs of
that society. The religious rituals on the other hand, would
represent the control mechanisms, both negative and positive,
by which a society governed its members.

In terms of the beliefs and rituals of this projected
"cult of man" Durkheim is unspecific. Besides an increasing
use of science (which Durkheim also sees as an outgrowth of
the Christian separation of the spiritual and the temporal)
in the belief systems, he suggests that the divine "humanity"
in each person will be "invested with that mysterious property
which creates an empty space around holy objects which keeps
them away from profane contacts and draws them from ordinary
life" (Ibid.:21). Durkheim also states, somewhat grandiosely:
"Its first dogma is the autonomy of reason and its first rite
the freedom of thought" (Ibid.:24).

Finally, in the cognitive or interpretive realm, this
cult of the future would find itself guided and influenced by
social science:

> Although faith, under the pressure of practical needs
> always had to anticipate science and complete it pre-
> maturely, Durkheim predicted that an increasingly
> rationalized and secularized religion would become
> ever more subject to the criticism and control of
> science. (Lukes, 1975:477)

This latter statement has a bearing on what Durkheim called the "cognitive" aspects of religious expression. In an age increasingly dominated by rationality, science and social science, religion could no longer be expected to fulfill a cognitive or interpretative function, explaining society to its members. Instead, social science would take over this role and be incorporated into the religious belief system in a sort of uneasy dialogue with faith.

Durkheim felt that although the "cult of man" would function to celebrate individualism, it would also function to restrict and control the individual. Hence it would not "indulge our instincts -- it offers us an ideal which surpasses nature" (Durkheim, 1969:24). Authority would still be respected if it was rationally based. Submission would be on the basis of recognized inadequacy. In the face of the lassitude and the despondency which marks the aftermath of a breakthrough in civil or social liberties, the "cult of man" would ritually guide the individuals involved so that they make best use of the hard-won liberties, to societies' advantage (Ibid.:29). In so regulating human behavior, these "cults of man" would be performing the same function as religion in the traditional societies. The difference would lie in the focus of this regulation: the defense of individual rights and liberties would be of paramount importance to the new cults.

These predictions about the future of religion, couched as they are in the form of an impassioned defense of individual liberties, fail to provide an operational definition of the "cult of man." Considered, however, in the light of Durkheim's basic hypotheses about the nature of religion, the picture becomes somewhat clearer. For instance, given Durkheim's hypothesis that the structure of society will causally shape the structure of that society's religious beliefs, it seems reasonable to predict that as society becomes more differentiated and specialized, so will religion. Implicit in Durkheim's work is the suggestion that one all-encompassing religion providing total integration will increasingly be replaced by a variety of religions. As more and more people come to feel they have nothing in common but their human individuality, religions will be based on the

belief that the idealized individual is sacred. Groups may
still vary in their image of the ideal man, as groups vary in
cultural and economic background, but the theme will be the
same.

This point has implications for a theory of recruitment.
In a highly specialized, differentiated society, a variety of
groups exist. Those most attracted to the "cult of man"
groups (as opposed to other religious groups) should be those
most affected by the sense of having "nothing in common."
They will be those, according to Durkheim, who are part of
the occupational structure in a highly specialized job, but
who (we may hypothesize) do not have other primary reference
groups to provide identity.

On the representational level, these groups will provide
their adherents with motivation and morals as well as with a
chance to dramatize their relations to society through
religious rituals. Science and/or social science will act as
interpreter, however, and so one may expect the belief
systems of such groups to be a mixture of the metaphoric
(expressive) and the scientific (explanatory) perhaps
expressing a tendency towards early closure and hence
simplification of available scientific ideas.

Finally, in terms of the functions of religion, in the
future Durkheim expected to find ritual ordering and
regulating social relations as in traditional religion. The
question of social order in the future was one that concerned
Durkheim greatly. The problem that disturbed him initially
was how, in a society that allowed for increasing individual
freedom of thought and action, would order be maintained.
His answer, that people would maintain order through the
defense of these individual rights and liberties, only partly
solved the problem. There still remained the question of how
authority would be established and maintained in such a
society. Who would be given the right to command and who
would follow?

As all such structural problems are, according to
Durkheim, expressed or reflected in the religion of the group,
we can see how pertinent this issue was in his projections
about the "cult of man." If all men had equal access to the
sacred, as they must in a cult which holds the idealized human

individual sacred, the process of establishing authority and submission is especially problematic. Durkheim suggests that authority will be rationally decided on the basis of competence and submission on the basis of incompetence (Durkheim, 1969). As Durkheim's study of primitive religions suggests that authority and control patterns are most vividly expressed by religious rituals, we may presume that competence and incompetence will therefore be determined in the rituals of these new cults. Hence we may also predict that in the cult of man religious rituals will involve skill development and skill testing of a progressive nature. As one becomes more ritually skilled, one will gain in authority.

In sum, then, it is important to note that Durkheim's predictions concerning religion in the future allow for the possible coexistence of a variety of different religions (and certainly cover the possibility of an increasingly specialized and differentiated society). The theme running through these various movements will be the sacredness of the ideal human. People will still feel a need to join in groups to dramatize these beliefs and the social realities which underlie them, and to be empowered and "morally remade" by this group interaction.

Since the late 1960's, a variety of new religious movements have appeared in North America, many of which would appear to fit Durkheim's description of the "cult of man." These movements have been heralded as a phenomenon distinct from the sects which American Protestantism has traditionally spawned. Their membership is largely middle class and so defied accepted economic-deprivation recruitment theories. Their rituals and beliefs are also distinct; many influenced by imported "eastern" religions. As a result, a variety of sociological and psychological theories have sprung up to explain the appearance of these groups. Before examining the groups themselves in the light of Durkheim's theory, these alternate theories will be explored.

CHAPTER II

ALTERNATIVE THEORIES: A QUEST FOR AN AMERICAN CULTURE

The existing literature on new religious movements falls
into two categories. On the one hand are those studies
concerned only with providing an ethnographic description of
particular groups and on the other are those studies (which
may or may not be informed by empirical observation) which
present theoretical explanations for the emergence of these
groups in modern society. In order to appreciate the
uniqueness of Durkheim's theory (and, generally, to illustrate
the need for a sociological theory in this area), this chapter
will be concerned only with reviewing the studies that fall
into this second category. Almost all of these studies derive
from one of three different theoretical traditions.

The "Counter-Culture" Hypothesis

Observers of new religious movements of the seventies
agree on two facts: one is that these groups recruit not
from the margins of society but from the young middle class
(Wuthnow, 1976a) and the other is that the doctrines, at
first glance, seem a radical break with the utilitarian
individualism which has been so central in forming and
maintaining the American way of life.

These two observations led to the development of the
counter-culture theory. According to this theory, which is,
in fact, an extension of the theories developed in the
sixties to account for the hippie-commune movements of that
era, American society is a spiritual wasteland. Based on
such works as Rozak's Making of a Counterculture (1969) and
Slater's Pursuit of Loneliness (1970), this theory suggests
that the youth of today (in particular the middle class
youth) are rejecting: (1) traditional Western acquisitive
and economic values; (2) role-orientated interpersonal
(bureaucratic) relationships; (3) isolationist, competitive
living; (4) rational, non-mystical thought; (5) structure or
standardization and mechanization (Prince, 1975:263). The
reason for this rejection has been variously explained by a

need to reproduce the early "expressive" milieu of the family
(Berger, 1970), a need to compensate for the unfeeling
bureaucracy (Adler, 1975), and a general socio-emotional
deprivation (Anthony and Robbins, 1975:479).

It is further argued that the "hippie" movement which
tried to produce a sense of togetherness through drugs and
street living, turned sour because relationships based on
the acquisition and consumption of drugs became as
instrumental as any in the larger society (Anthony and
Robbins, 1975). So adherents turned to new religious movements, hoping for another crack at developing and experiencing
a more expressive communal milieu.

Consistent with this theory is the fact that the
membership of many, if not most of these groups, has been
shown to be composed, at least in part, of dropouts from the
drug "scene" (Anthony and Robbins, 1975; Tobey, 1976; Johnson,
1976; Wuthnow, 1976a). Secondly, there is a doctrinal
emphasis in many of these groups on the "oneness" of all
creation, on communal living and on the non-rational.

Nevertheless, the assumptions of this theory have not
been borne out by subsequent data collected on a variety of
these new religious movements. Few of these groups appear to
offer adherents either a non-instrumental milieu or a viable
alternative to the dominant American lifestyle. For instance,
the four most popular groups (in terms of participation)
(Wuthnow, 1976a) are TM, Yoga, est and Tongues (Charismatic
Renewal). The first three are all offered on a consumer
basis. The new member pays for a course and then practices
the learned skills alone. No group life of any duration is
offered. Nor can the beliefs of these groups be seen as
counter-cultural. TM and est self-consciously advertise
themselves as techniques to aid adherents in achieving success
and personal happiness as traditionally defined. Charismatic
groups, while they do offer a sense of community (Westley,
1977; McGuire, 1975) are in no way counter-cultural. Members
are nearly always devout Protestants or Catholics to begin
with and continue to adhere to traditional belief systems in
the context of the new group (Harrison, 1974).

Finally, even those less popular groups which seem to be
both communal and counter-cultural in nature (Hare Krishna

being possibly the best example) do not provide warm or affective relationships (Johnson, 1976:45). Hence, the "counter-cultural" theory has not been borne out by the data. In an effort in part to side-step this discrepancy between theory and fact, a second theory has evolved which may be called the "cultural crisis" hypothesis.

The "Cultural Crisis" Hypothesis

This theory, which is a modification of its predecessor, postulates that the new religious movements of the seventies arose because of a "cultural crisis" in North American society, brought on by the breakdown of the accepted meaning systems and orientations.

All human beings, this theory suggests, have a need for accepted definitions and explanations of human existence and such phenomena as evil, death and suffering. These explanations were formerly considered real and absolute. In this century, however, people have increasingly seen that such codes were socially constructed and therefore purely relative (Eister, 1975:619).

This realization, it is argued, has led on the one hand to a sense of dislocation (a sort of cultural identity crisis experienced acutely on the individual level) and on the other hand, to a sense of freedom in the search for new orientations ("doing your own thing").

The new religious movements, it is suggested, are a response expressive of both sentiments. They represent an abandonment of science and social science, which have proved inadequate explanations of the purpose of life, and a 'hunger for a new psychology' (Needleman, 1970). These movements purpose to relocate and reorientate adherents from the outer to the inner world. For this reason the 'self' has taken on a nearly sacred quality as the "ens realissimum of the human being" (Berger, 1973:416). Impulse is glorified as the voice of this inner Self (Turner, 1976). The rituals of the movement "allow for improvisation of new roles and the institutionalization of the self, of modulating affect and of establishing points of personal anchorage and orientation" (Adler, 1975:284).

But the realization of the relativity of social facts has opened new horizons as well as creating disorientation. The groups offer people a chance to escape the bonds of rationality or "material reality" imposed for so long by science. They emphasize, to this end, the irrational and the unseen, while using scientific language. They thus offer a more inclusive and satisfying meaning system (Whitehead, 1975; Tiryakian, 1974; Glock, 1976).

In sum, then, the "cultural crisis" theory suggests that the new religious movements of the seventies arose in response to a breakdown of meaning systems and of the orientational institutions responsible for their formulation and maintenance. The groups offer adherents (who may be seen as suffering from meaning deprivation) new meaning systems, which both supply a new sense of location and a wider, more inclusive vision of human experience unrestricted by science or rationality.

This theory offers a viable explanation for the very private nature of rituals in these groups (after all, focus on self is a private business) but it has, nonetheless, several important weaknesses.

In the first place, the idea that people join these groups as a response to meaning deprivation, and indeed that such deprivation exists, is questionable. Indeed, the one study to make use of any substantial amount of empirical data, suggests that people do not experiment with new religious movements in order to find meaning, rather they experiment because they are already committed to a meaning system which advocates such experimentation (Wuthnow, 1976b).

Secondly, if, in fact, members were in search of explanations about human existence, we would expect them to value the ideas which the groups present to their adherents, rather than the practices and/or claimed results of those practices. In fact, the opposite appears to be the case. Adherents of the most popular groups (again, TM, Yoga and such groups as est) polled in a recent survey at Concordia University in Montreal, stated that they joined the group because of its claimed results and practices more than twice as often as they stated that they joined because of the groups' ideas (Bird, 1978). Trainees attending sessions of

est, one of the fastest growing cults in America, receive a
uniform answer to all demands for explanations: "Because it
works" (Bry, 1976).

Lastly, while traditional rituals deal mainly with the
kind of fundamental questions (birth, death, puberty,
suffering) with which the "cultural crisis" theory is
concerned, there is a conspicuous absence of this focus in
rituals in these new religious movements (Bird, 1978). In
many cases there is no effort to connect rituals that do
exist, such as meditation or physical postures, with any
overarching cosmology.

The Anti-Cultural Hypothesis

The third theory to emerge, partially in response to or
in criticism of the above two theories is the "anti-cultural"
hypothesis. Not only do these movements fail to challenge
the prevailing ethos of American society, it is argued, they
are part and parcel of the general moral decline and
disintegration which marks that society.

Proponents of this hypothesis suggest that not only is
the work world instrumental but even today's family offers no
expressive or affective milieu, but rather "an unparallelled
flight from intimacy" (Lasch, 1975). Relationships on all
levels are seen as becoming increasingly superficial; people
are preoccupied only with themselves. Even this preoccupation, expressed as it is in sociopsychological jargon
(which the cultural-crisis theory deemed expressive of a new
awareness) is superficial "psychobabble" which "deludes many
people into thinking they need not examine themselves with
anything but its dull instrument ... it anaesthetizes
curiosity, numbs the desire to know" (Rosen, 1976:49).

Placed in this general picture of the increasing disintegration of the cultural and moral fabric of North America,
new religious movements emerge as yet another manifestation of
"the new narcissism" centered "solely on the self and with
individual survival as its sole good ... a retreat from the
worlds of morality and history, an unembarrassed denial of
human reciprocity and communication" (Marin, 1975:46). Their
members' tendencies towards egotism and privatism are seen as
not counter-cultural but "anti-cultural" spelling the doom of
religion and society:

> They indicate the extent to which religion has become inconsequential for modern society. They have no real consequences for other social institutions, for political power structures, for technological constraints or controls. They add nothing to any prospective reintegration of society and contribute nothing toward the culture by which a society might live. (Wilson, 1976:96)

In sum, the anti-cultural theory suggests that these groups reflect the pathological tendency towards narcissism of contemporary society. They offer adherents a chance to take refuge in rituals which formalize this self-preoccupation.

While this theory provides an antidote to the sometimes naive optimism of the counter-culture and cultural crisis theories, it is, nevertheless, flawed in two respects. Firstly, it rests on a questionable psychological assumption that the privatistic orientation of belief and ritual of the new groups reflects an individual pathological condition of self-preoccupation and inability to relate to others. Secondly, this assumption is used as a basis to draw the equally questionable sociological conclusion that these groups represent a disintegrative social trend, and provide nothing in the way of public shared belief.

In order to be considered a religion, a group must have some conception of transcendence, even if only a conception of an inner spiritual Being who transcends the limitations of external reality. An inner focus may be seen as narcissistic if the preoccupation is with the contemplators' own material body and personality, but if contemplation on an inner transcendent may be called narcissism, then many of the great Eastern traditions may be so termed as well as some varieties of ascetic Protestantism. An example of the latter are the Amish and Mennonites, whose notion of salvation is internal and personal and could in many ways be seen as selfish. It is considered idolatrous to invest too much emotion in things and people of the world; all energy should be directed to love of God and the soul's salvation. Of course, implicit in this notion of salvation is the conception of dispassionate love of fellows and careful observance of the rules of social interaction and obligation. The means is therefore a highly cohesive community, but the ends may well be seen as

individualistic and self-orientated: the salvation of the
soul within.

If this is true it suggests that an inner preoccupation
does not preclude the possibility of a reaffirmation of
social bonds. The matter hinges on whether the inner contemplation focuses merely on the self or whether the notion
of salvation extends to include transpersonal and interpersonal relations. The fact that new religious groups are
groups joining people together in a common pursuit argues
that their concerns surpass those of mere narcissism. Even
the most extreme new religious movement which makes no
mention of God and dwells on the purely human does not dwell
on the purely individual. Some concept of transcendent
humanity is included.

While these groups may not provide the utopian brother-
love envisioned by the counter-culture theorists and/or even
the cohesive communities of the ascetic Protestant groups,
the evidence is that those groups most accused of narcissism
(such as est, TM) do not make world rejecting mystics out of
their membership. Quite the contrary, they seem to tie them
more firmly to the world (Tipton, 1977; Stone, 1976; Wallis,
1977). The bonds which are reaffirmed may be the cold
"instrumental" bonds of bureaucracy, but they remain bonds.
Indeed some of these groups seem to lend these bonds new
strength by colouring them with expressive meaning. For
instance, a careful study of one group, the Meyer Baba group,
suggests that it acts to resuscitate members so that they can
continue to perform effectively. To this end, the group
"legitimates expressive role orientations for adults ... the
cult's ethic incorporates the instrumental values which allow
it to perpetuate itself within the larger society while
maintaining the expressive emphasis which gave it birth"
(Anthony and Robbins, 1975:511).

In sum, then, while the "anti-cultural" theories
recognize the unique privatistic and introspective nature of
many new religious movements, by using psychological
variables as a basis for making sociological generalizations,
they fail to recognize either the bonds that continue to
exist between people or the new bonds being formed. Secondly,
they fail to recognize that when the ideal of human potential

is shared by a group of people, it cannot be treated as mere
individual narcissism but must be seen as reflecting some
aspects of social relations, collective views of man and
society.

Summary and Conclusions

In sum, the theories concerning new religious movements
have evolved from an optimistic to a pessimistic perspective.
The overt characteristics which seem to make these groups
unique (such as belief systems which seem to emphasize the
divine self within, a seeming emphasis on the "oneness" of
all, and on communal, non-institutionalized relations) and
which were initially heralded as counter-cultural, were
gradually interpreted as compensatory. Finally, the
realization of the essentially privatistic experiential
nature of these rituals and groups produced the anti-cultural
theory based on a psychological interpretation of members as
narcissistic, frightened, maladaptive and irrational.

We have suggested specific weaknesses of the foregoing
theories. We will conclude by stating a general weakness of
all three. These theories suggest that religion is performing a compensatory role -- providing members either with
an alternative to the dominant ethos, a chance to establish
a meaning system where none existed before, or a chance to
escape and ignore society's problems through a preoccupation
with the inner self.

As compensatory theories, they all include a hypothesis
about the subjective experience which creates these needs.
In all three cases, this is done purely theoretically; there
is little evidence provided that such needs and moods exist
in society at large. The logic of these constructions seems
to be as follows: these groups self-consciously advertize
themselves as providing 'x' (say community). Therefore, it
is hypothesized, members must need 'x'. Therefore, society
at large must be deficient in 'x'. When closer study reveals
that groups, while advertising themselves as providing 'x',
in fact provide 'y' (privatization) theorists shift either to
persist that since society is deficient in 'x' then the groups
are dysfunctional, causing further disintegration, or else
shift their focus from the society to the individual and

postulate that the individual is hiding from this deficiency
in the rituals of the groups. What remains unestablished is
this original deficiency: 'x'.

In sum, these theories seem to be built more in response
to each other and to the need to make a larger statement
about American culture than from the empirical data. In the
process they have failed to give a coherent explanation of
the idiosyncracies of these groups which first attracted
interest, such as their middle class membership. The theories
also fail to reveal the complexity of beliefs and rituals
which these new groups represent.

Durkheim's theory provides a much more refined instrument
for examining these groups. Instead of focusing on the larger
society, it focuses on the group beliefs and rituals. It
allows for the possibility that these cults are not compensatory at all but rather expressive of members' experiences.
In addition, Durkheim suggests that such cults need not be
expressive of all of society, but only those parts which
members experience.

Hence, Durkheim's theory allows for an explanation of
recruitment patterns and of the particular beliefs and rituals
of these cults. Because Durkheim has articulated rather
precise criteria for his "cult of man," it also allows us to
make initial distinctions between groups. It must be noted,
finally, that a major failing of all three of the above
theories is that they fail to differentiate between the
variety of new religious movements which have sprung up in
the seventies. One of the first steps in understanding them
is to articulate their differences.

The remainder of this thesis will therefore be concerned
with an analysis of data on new religious movements using
Durkheim's theory as an analytic tool to examine and interpret
various aspects of these groups and the way they articulate
aspects of the social structure.

In particular, of course, we will focus on those new
religious movements which, at least in their external form,
fit Durkheim's description of the "cult of man."

CHAPTER III

DATA AND METHODOLOGY

The data used in this thesis was gathered over a period of five years by fifteen different researchers in the Department of Religion at Concordia University in Montreal. The project was funded by a grant from the Quebec government (FCAC), and co-directed by Professor Frederick Bird from the Department of Religion and Professor Bill Reimer from the Department of Sociology.

The researchers themselves were graduate students, largely involved in advanced studies in comparative religion. In any given year (the project lasted from the Fall of 1973 until the Spring of 1978) the research team vascillated in size, at its maximum involving seven students (1975-76) at the minimum three (1977-78). The author participated for three years (1975-78) both as researcher and as co-administrator.

The research procedure was as follows: a researcher would select a new religious movement in the Montreal area in which she was interested and/or had contacts. The researcher would enter the group, attend weekly meetings and familiarize herself sufficiently with the organizational format and membership to fill out a standardized Survey Index Form developed by the team (see Appendix). She would then request permission to interview core members of the group. If this permission was granted by the leadership of the group, she would then obtain a list of the core membership. A random sample of the core membership would then be selected from this list. These individuals would in turn be contacted for interviews, and if they agreed to be interviewed, a standard (formal) interview schedule (see Appendix) would be administered. This interview was fairly long, modelled on a similar interview developed by Glock and Wuthnow (Wuthnow, 1976b) in conjunction with a similar project at University of California, Berkeley. In addition, Lofland's conversion model was built into the schedule, with questions designed to

21

For purposes of this dissertation, only a fraction of this data has been utilized: that pertaining to groups which may be defined as "cult of man" groups. There are six such groups in this sample, Shakti, Silva Mind Control, Psychosynthesis, Arica, est and Scientology.

Earlier it was noted that one of the problems concerning the theoretical approaches to new religious movements has been the failure to differentiate between different kinds of movements. Initially, theorists such as Ellwood (1973) and Needleman (1970) omitted completely the new Christian groups such as the Catholic Charismatics, Jesus Freaks, and Children of God, which in fact accounted for a large proportion of the "religious revival" (Wuthnow, 1976a; Bird, 1978). In the case of Needleman, this bias seems due to what he felt were the transformative possibilities of the emphasis on "unity of being" of many of the "eastern" groups. Closer inspection of this sample, however, indicated that some bore the stamp of western occult tradition (long borrowers of eastern ideas) and western transpersonal psychology, while others seemed much more recent imports. Recently, a number of typologies have been developed (most notably Anthony and Robbins, 1978; Bird, 1978; Wuthnow, 1976a; Glock and Bellah, 1976; Wilson, 1976). These typologies conflict considerably. The neo-Christian groups tend to emerge regularly as a distinct group but there is some disagreement about classifying the remaining groups which all seem to be more or less influenced by eastern beliefs and practices, more or less by western occult and transpersonal psychology. They group differently according to whether the practices, beliefs or organization is selected as a point of reference.

In narrowing our own focus and selecting the above six groups, we have chosen to follow Durkheim's own directive and select on the basis of the most "exterior and apparent form" (Durkheim, 1899:16). For Durkheim, the most apparent feature of all religions and the one he selects for closest examination in his discussion of the "cult of man" is the definition of the sacred. It is the conception of the sacred which reflects the "collectively conceived" as opposed to the profane which reflects "that which is individually conceived and the result of quite naked individual impressions" (Lukes,

1975:242). From this conception of the sacred will flow the relationships between organization ritual and belief which were Durkheim's concern as well as ours.

In locating six groups as potential representatives of the "cult of man" we have used the simple criterion that they should hold the human individual as sacred. While this focus fails to produce an exhaustive typology of new religious movements, it does highlight two types of groups: those which clearly locate the sacred as lying within the human individual and those which clearly locate the sacred as lying outside the human individual. These groups must, however, be seen as points at two ends of a continuum; they are joined by a variety of movements whose view of the sacred is more ambiguous. Even among our six groups, there is some variety, usually in the degree at which the limits of human potential are set. Groups like Shakti and Scientology see all things as possible to the developed human being to the point of defying the laws of time and space. A group like est does not make such grandiose claims, while not precluding them either in their statements that the individual is the "cause" of everything that happens to him (no matter what positivistic explanations are available). The margins of the "type" are also not distinct. However, all these groups claim access to superhuman powers for all members, within all members (as opposed to occult groups which manipulate powers outside themselves). The leaders of these groups are not seen as being any more divine than their followers (unlike many groups like Divine Light Mission and the Moonies who see their leaders as incarnate dieties). The leaders may have developed more of their potential, but the potential is shared by all human beings.

This common definition of the sacred has caused these groups to be labelled human potential groups by some theorists. They share many beliefs and organizational features which will be dealt with at length in the body of this dissertation. However, on the basis of this one characteristic, their location of the sacred within the human individual, we shall tentatively label them "cult of man" groups. The object of this dissertation will be to explore the details of belief, organization and ritual within these groups to try to establish if the other elements which Durkheim predicted would be linked to such a belief are in fact present, as compared to those groups without such a belief.

Obviously, this exploration can in no sense be defended as a test of Durkheim's predictions. Our "cult of man" sample is in no respect random and may or may not be representational. This is equally true of the group selected for comparative purposes, the Catholic Charismatic Renewal movement. It was selected not because it is necessarily representational but because it clearly locates the sacred outside the individual and because the Concordia project has the most complete data on this movement of all new religious groups with such a belief. The author herself has participated in one chapter of this movement for a period of four months and conducted four interviews. Ten other interviews are available (as well as a total of two years of fieldnotes) from two other chapters in the Montreal area.

The author has also participated in a Silva Mind Control group (coursework and interview over four months), a Psychosynthesis group (coursework and interviews over five months) and conducted the interviews with Arica members and the est member. Material on Scientology, Shakti are drawn from the interviews and fieldnotes of other researchers.[1]

Finally, in Chapters V and VI, we use data on turn-of-the-century cults as historical counterbalance to these contemporary groups. This data is entirely drawn from secondary sources which will be identified in the text.

SECTION II

THE RELATIONSHIP OF BELIEFS AND SOCIAL
ORGANIZATION IN "CULT OF MAN" GROUPS

Earlier we have noted that Durkheim's view of the
religion of the future was that it would reflect the diversity
and plurality of modern industrial society. He abandoned the
notion of religion as the overarching, conceptual system,
insisting, nevertheless, that Man would continue to need to
express himself in symbolic terms, and to establish his link
to society through religion.

This notion of Durkheim's casts a very different light on
the study of religion in North America, than that espoused by
many contemporary theorists. Following the focus on the
"secularization" trend, both Wilson (1976) and Fenn (1972)
attack the notion that the new religious movements can have
any theoretical importance. Both suggest that never again can
religion provide any kind of societal integration. Wilson
suggests the new movements offer nothing of general value to
North American society; Fenn indicates that with increasing
rise in problems of unemployment, the problem will be one of
reducing motivation, of disengaging people rather than trying
to maximize social solidarity. There will be less and less
place for religion.

When Fenn or Wilson dismiss the new religious movements
as of little significance, they are in fact dismissing
religion as of little significance, which for Durkheim would
be the equivalent of dismissing the relation of social
organization to collective ideas. Because both the systems
of religious beliefs and of social organization are fragmented
and pluralistic does not indicate that essential relationship
between the two has disappeared, nor that this relationship
should no longer be of essential concern to sociologists.
The danger of the secularization theory and those who dismiss
new religions as being of little significance because they
are fragmentary manifestations is that they mistake change for
disappearance, and therefore abandon the subject when what is

27

called for is the development of different instruments to measure and define. It seems ironic that at a time of crucial shift in ethics and morality, theorists should abandon the study of that phenomenon which for Durkheim was the basis whereby other collective representations such as law and morality might be interpreted (Durkheim, 1899).

The fact that Durkheim did suggest that modern religion might be diverse and fragmented offers the student of modern religion the opportunity to look at the new religious movements comparatively while still employing Durkheim's notions of the relationships between belief and social structure. Groups may be compared with each other in their basic dimensions of belief, organization and ritual and they may further be singly compared to the larger North American culture of which they are a part. This latter comparison is of particular interest. While Durkheim's basic tenet was that collective representations or beliefs were a reflection of the social organization from which they emerged, he also granted these beliefs a kind of autonomy. He felt that religious beliefs often grew and proliferated in relation to each other and not in a one-to-one correspondence to features of the social organization:

> ... they (ideas) have the power to attract and repel
> each other and to form amongst themselves various
> syntheses, which are determined by their natural
> affinities and not by the state of the environment
> in the midst of which they evolve. (Durkheim, 1953:31)

In addition, Durkheim also held that beliefs (collective) once formed could in turn influence the social organization of society. His concern was as much with the interaction between social structure and social consciousness as with their causal relationship (Lukes, 1975:226-236).

The study of new religious movements gives us a unique arena in which to study this interaction. Each group has its own beliefs which may be determined by either the social structure of the wider North American culture, or by the social structure of the individual group. On the other hand, these beliefs once formulated may in turn influence the social structure of both the individual group and the larger social organization. What we have then is a system of feedback between beliefs and social structure on two levels:

macrocosm and microcosm.

This interaction is particularly crucial at times of social change. If changes in the social structure of North American society produce changes in the dominant religious symbol system, we must presume this takes place over time. It is conceivable, therefore, that at a point in time in the change process, the beliefs will still be representing an outmoded social structure, one which has disappeared. However, if at the same time a small group has developed within the new larger social structure, similar in structure to that larger organization, it may produce beliefs which represent the larger social structure better than the currently held "dominant" belief systems. If this were the case, it might be hypothesized that these new beliefs held by the small group will be of considerably more importance in the larger social structure than the size of the group in which they originated might lead us to believe.

Hence, it is difficult to evaluate the importance of any religious movement solely on the basis of its membership size, particularly in modern times when the mass media does such a good job of disseminating information about social movements and their ideologies. What we must first do is to look closer at the relationship between group beliefs and social organization.

We are concerned first to locate our "cult of man" sample historically and sociologically. In Chapter IV, the historical antecedents of the "cult of man" groups will be outlined. In Chapter V, the social structure of the groups themselves will be examined in comparison to (a) the Catholic Charismatics, a new religious group which has a radically different view of the sacred than the "cult of man" groups, and (b) the turn-of-the-century occult and healing cults to which these "cult of man" groups are historically related. In Chapter VI, a similar comparison will be carried out, this time involving the specific beliefs which flow from the structural elements discussed in Chapter V. Finally, Chapter VII will return to an examination of the "cult of man" groups themselves, focusing on the way the specific beliefs discussed in Chapter VI relate to the central conception of the sacred and the way in which these beliefs

mirror the members' experience in the larger North American
social structure.

CHAPTER IV

THE "CULT OF MAN": HISTORICAL ANTECEDENTS AND
CONTEMPORARY PERSPECTIVES

The "human potential movement" is a term which covers a
wide range of groups. Stone (1976) has included under that
heading encounter groups, gestalt awareness training, transactional analysis, sensory awareness, primal therapy, bio-
energetics, massage, Psychosynthesis, humanistic psychology,
est, Arica, psychic healing, biofeedback and Silva Mind
Control. Some of these are clearly in the realm of straightforward therapy groups which cannot by any stretch of the
imagination be termed religious; others appear to be
techniques as opposed to movements. There are among them,
however, a number of groups which have been labelled "transpersonal trainings" which Stone argues offers a "more
elaborated world view or theology than encounter or bodily
disciplines" (Stone, 1976:97). These groups correspond to
our "cult of man" sample: Arica, est, Psychosynthesis, and
Silva Mind Control. Stone notes that they are among the
fastest growing of all contemporary movements, having doubled
in size each year since 1970. In 1974, Arica claimed 20,000
graduates, est claimed 30,000, Psychosynthesis claimed 1,000
(Ibid.:98).

The common ground for all human potential movements,
interpersonal or transpersonal, is, according to Stone,
"gestalt consciousness and its perception that reality is not
as 'hard' as it seems to be. What was once a fixation or a
historical fact becomes very malleable. Following on this is
the realization that reality is personally constructed and
reconstructed all the time" (Ibid., 1976:106). However,
while gestalt therapy is aware of the human mind as the
active agent in the construction of reality, and suggests as
a heuristic device that human possibilities are limitless,
the transpersonal groups in fact elaborate this insight into
a philosophical system, which makes them, of all the new
religious movements of the seventies, the closest to
Durkheim's "cult of man." All of these groups share a central

belief: that the human being has two parts, an 'ego' or
'personality' that acts in the world and a Higher Self,
Essence or Being that transcends the world. This higher self
is seen as a piece of divinity ... a literally limitless
potential of man, and the techniques of these groups center
around the development of this potential.

In addition to the four groups which Stone classed as
"transpersonal," we have also included two groups not
mentioned by Stone. The first of these is Scientology, which
Stone no doubt omitted because it is one of the "groups that
exert strong pressure for organizational loyalty or orthodoxy
of belief or ritual" which Stone felt barred a group from the
rather open format of all other human potential movements.
In many respects, this feature of Scientology also makes it
unlike the "cult of man," which Durkheim conceived as a loose
association. However, its concept of the sacred nature of
the human being, embodied in the notion of the 'Operating
Thetan', is similar to that of the "cult of man" and for that
reason, we will include some references to this group. The
second group, not mentioned by Stone but included here, is
Shakti, a group of very small numbers but which has a chapter
in Montreal. Below is a summary of each of these six groups:

Scientology: Founded in 1952 by L. Ron Hubbard, this
group is a direct outgrowth of Dianetics, Hubbard's
first group. Scientology offers a graded hierarchy
of courses, of a quasi-therapeutic and highly 'technical' nature,designed to release fully the
individual's superhumanly powerful inner potential
and eliminate most human weaknesses such as illness,
incompetence and insecurity. The organization is
highly centralized and bureaucratized. The courses
are expensive and marketed with sophisticated sales
techniques. Size is difficult to estimate but the
movement is international and capable of maintaining
numerous centres, a permanent staff and a fleet of
vessels, on which Ron Hubbard lives,called "The Sea
Org."

Psychosynthesis: Founded in the second decade of this
century by an Italian psychiatrist, Roberto Assagioli.
Psychosynthesis spread to North America in the 1960's,
where it attracted many people who had a background in
the new therapies and growth disciplines such as
Gestalt, Transactional Analysis and the Encounter
Group movement. It's headquarters are presently
located in San Francisco, but there are branches in
Montreal, Europe and California. The emphasis of the
movement is on releasing constructive forces and

developing positive resources, includes a belief
in a transpersonal or higher self, which is distinct
from and transcends the personal self, and connects
the individual to the universal or collective unconscious. Students enter training either in personal
development or in order to become therapists themselves. Workshops and courses vary in length and
expense but average around ten dollars per session
for group work and thirty-five for individual.

Arica: An eclectic movement borrowing techniques
from Zen, Sufism, Buddhism, psychoanalysis, encounter
groups, gestalt, science fiction and Gurdgieff
traditions, this movement was founded by a South
American named Oscar Ichazo. Ichazo was a religious
seeker who experimented in a variety of traditions
in a variety of countries before starting his own in
the town of Arica, Chile. His first pupils were a
group of fifty Americans (among them, John Lilly)
who came to study with him for forty days for the
price of $1500 each. In 1971, the Arica Institute
opened in New York. The Montreal branch opened in
1977 with eight teachers. It offers a series of
programs lasting from one hour to 40 days and costing
from five to eight hundred dollars. The object of the
programs is "ego-reduction" based on technique/
experience, not on belief/faith. These techniques
involve personality assessment through a complex
series of enneagrams, movement exercises, meditation
and role playing games.

est: Standing for Erhard Seminar Training, est is a
personalized training in "experiencing your problem
and making it disappear." Founded in 1971 by Werner
Erhard, a student of Scientology, SMC and Mind
Dynamics and a business man, the course takes two
weekends and costs $250. It has become known for its
ordeal nature: participants pay to be harangued and
insulted by trainers, forced to sit for hours on hard
chairs with few bathroom or food breaks, vomit, faint
and claim that their lives are changed. The techniques include lectures, testimonials and imagination-
game playing exercises similar to Silva Mind Control.

Shakti: Termed by members, "the spiritual science of
DNA." Shakti was a religious movement which existed
in Montreal from April to December, 1973. It was one
of a series of religious movements planned, carried
out and closed down by a central religious organization in Crestline, California. Their founder and
director is E. J. Gold, the son of H. L. Gold, a
well-known science fiction writer in the 30's and 40's.
The religious movements have been established since
1968 under different names, in different cities of
North America, and offer a wide, constantly shifting
range of ideas, aims and techniques. They all share
the common features of eclecticism, humour, a great
variety of techniques, built-in obsolescence, and a
strong scientific and theatrical flavour. Underlying

these movements is a core philosophy of reincarnation, spiritual evolution and a shamanic search for power, knowledge and conscious control over the soul's destiny.

Silva Mind Control: Silva Mind Control was founded in the late sixties by José Silva, a Mexican-American, who became interested in psychic phenomena. The movement claims more than 50,000 graduates. Using scientific assumptions about brain-wave frequencies -- beta, alpha, theta, delta -- and associated "states of consciousness," SMC offers a basic week long course for approximately $150 which progresses from memory training, sleep, weight and habit control techniques, through projection of consciousness, telepathy, clairvoyance, psychic healings. The goal of the course is to make "acting psychics" out of its students. The movement stresses that the "greater powers" which the students develop must be used for the "betterment of mankind." Its adherents believe that the powers and abilities of the human mind are limitless.

The techniques, rituals, beliefs and social organizations of these groups have their origins in three different traditions in western culture. Stone has located them in the encounter group/gestalt therapy tradition and indeed all of these groups draw some techniques, particularly the role-playing and interactional rituals from this tradition. However, there are also elements, more or less stressed depending on the group, of two other traditions: the western occult/mystical tradition and the western positive thinking/healing tradition.

The western occult/mystical tradition is the oldest of these in historical terms. Ellwood (1973) has noted that since the time of Plato, this magical, eclectic and intellectual tradition has been the portal for eastern influences in western thought. In all cases leaders of such movements, from the early Orphic cults onwards, were seen as shamanistic figures, wanderers, usually familiar with Asia, who provided for their followers a secret knowledge revealed through techniques or processes and used for personal power. Ellwood traces this line of western thought through the gnostic movements of the Augustinian period, the witches, kabbalists and alchemists of the Middle Ages, the Rosicrucians of the Renaissance, the Freemasons and the Swedenborgians of the 18th century and the Harmonial movements of the early 20th century, such as the Theosophy

and I Am movements. Among other things that these movements
have contributed to contemporary "cult of man" groups are:

1. The Gnostic, Kaballistic and Pythagorean idea of
   pre- and post-existence in a spiritual state.

2. The Spiritualist idea of talk with persons on
   the other side.

3. A monistic idea of God.

4. A Gnostic idea of events of great importance
   transpiring in the invisible spiritual world
   known only to initiates.

5. Most significantly, the Second Coming of Christ
   which Swedenborg said happened spiritually in
   1757. His emphasis on this invisible con-
   sumation must be a precursor of modern "New Age"
   and "Aquarian Age" ideas.

6. The idea of the plurality of worlds, each with
   its own spirits and angels.

7. The Renaissance idea that God's Consciousness
   is continuous with man. (Ellwood, 1973:66)

The "cult of man" groups have adopted some of these
ideas, notably Nos. 1, 6 and 7, and developed them in their
own particular style (which will be discussed in greater
detail later).

A peculiar American twist was given to this mystical/
occult approach by the transcendentalists of the 19th century
led by Emerson. This profoundly romantic, albeit intellectual, movement focused on the idea of God's consciousness
as continuous with Man's. As Emerson said:

> It is the office of a true teacher to show us what
> God is, not was; all men go in flocks to this saint
> or that poet avoiding the God who seeth in secret.
> They think society wiser than their soul, and know
> not that one soul, and their soul, is wiser than
> the whole world. (Gaustad, 1974:142)

The wisdom of the soul became the wisdom of the mind for
the descendents of this movement: the positive-thought cults
of the early 20th century. Among these were New Thought,
Unity and Christian Science, whose leaders (Mary Baker Eddy,
Quimby) espoused the value of positive thought:

> The mind is capable of transcending all limitations
> the world seems to have placed around it because the
> mind is ultimately sovereign, or is all that is.

> Mind can enjoy communication with those who have
> seemed to die: mind can expand through intuitions
> to embrace the cosmos; mind can create by its own
> direct force all desirable conditions of life.
> (Ellwood, 1973:81)

These groups also put great emphasis on the healing powers of the mind and on the fact that danger, evil and illness were all due to faulty thinking, negative idea habits.

The "cult of man" groups draw a number of themes from this particular tradition. Among the most important is the intimate connection between the body and the mind; bodily conditions are often seen as direct reflection of mental states. The optimism inherent in the notion of positive thought, and its ability to shape the world, is particularly visible in a group like Silva Mind Control, although it is shared by most groups.

Finally, as mentioned, the "cult of man" groups have roots in the encounter group movement. Bach (1973) has traced the beginnings of the human potential movement to the work of Kurt Lewin in the late forties. In the process of conducting a series of group workshops for teachers in Connecticut, he developed what were to become the touchstones of the early movement, the concepts of feedback, group confrontation, encounter and process analysis (Bach, 1973:8).

The movement has gone through three stages since the late fifties. At first, the emphasis was on intense group confrontation in a kind of "cultural island," cut off from the normal activities of the trainees. Within this island, adherents found they had special 'change' experiences of considerable impact. The idea was that this experience would generalize to increasing leadership abilities. When it was discovered that in fact the experience did not seem to generalize, an evolution in focus began. This next period witnessed a slow shift from the group emphasis to a more individual emphasis.

> ... There was a period around the middle '50's
> when there was quite a struggle going on between
> east and west around the individual and the group
> emphasis ... as I see it now, there is much more
> of an individual emphasis in sensitivity training
> now than there is in the original group emphasis.
> (Ibid.:61)

Finally, in the early sixties, Mike Murphy, a psychology graduate student from Stanford, who had travelled extensively in the east before becoming familiar with the encounter group movement in California, decided to open a centre which would combine these two types of knowledge. He founded Esalen, and in the process, took the encounter group movement even further from its original concerns with group life to the development of the individual through group life. At least one of the basic ideas of the Esalen system was very similar to the general T-group theory -- a series of group sessions without agenda, directed toward interaction and reaction among members as the main topic. The Esalen-type system, however, does not aim at training people for group activity. The watchwords are personal growth, expansion of human potentiality and encounter (Ibid.:66).

The final figure of importance to the encounter group movement was Carl Rogers (WBSl -- counselling psychology), who further developed the concept of the unique powers of the individual.

> Rogers worked out the ideological implications ... these consisted of a deep-seated conviction that each person has his own intrinsic value and that his individuality should be respected. The non-directive counselor, therefore, would not force his own therapeutic convictions on the client, but would only help him to reach his own potential. (Ibid.:67)

In sum, the encounter group movement has moved in twenty years from group to self, and from self to transcendental self. Bach has argued that the experience of change and growth, which could be elicited from the kind of group interaction established by the early encounter groups, was akin to religious ecstacy as opposed to scientific experiment. Due to this paradox, the movement has always been plagued by a split between scientists and humanists. At the moment it is the humanists who seem to have gained control of the movement, and it is certainly to this branch of the organization that the "cult of man" groups are indebted. The influence of this tradition is still seen in the heavily social-scientific language used by many of the movements, notably Psychosynthesis and Arica and the rationalized "coursework format," for which

members pay a set fee. As noted earlier, interaction
exercises, role-playing feedback and process evaluation are
still present in some of these groups, but as we shall see,
are being used for distinctly different ends than those for
which they were originally intended.

In sum, the groups we have included as "cult of man"
groups seem a mixture of the late stages of the human
potential movement, the positive-thought movement and the
occult traditions. The point of agreement of all three of
these is that it is the human individual who is seen as
sacred, as all powerful. This sacred power is seen as located
deep within the individual personality. Actions in the outer
world become significant, not in themselves, but only in terms
of their impact on this inner self.

We shall pick up these various ideological strands in
greater detail in Chapter VI. In the next chapter, however,
we will leave for a moment the ideological underpinnings of
"cult of man" groups and look instead at the organizational
elements which distinguish them. From a Durkheimian
perspective, it is these elements which are of paramount
importance, for from them will flow both beliefs and rituals.

CHAPTER V

DISTINGUISHING ORGANIZATIONAL FEATURES OF "CULT OF MAN" GROUPS: A COMPARATIVE VIEW

For Durkheim, religious beliefs were "collective
representations" which drew their "nature and power" largely
from "the way in which the associated individuals are
grouped." He argued that the source of these representations
must come from something "outside them":

> Either the collective conscience floats in the void
> like a sort of inconceivable absolute, or it is
> connected with the rest of the world through the
> intermediary of a substratum on which, in consequence
> it depends. On the other hand, of what can this
> substratum be composed if not of the members of
> society as they are socially combined? (Durkheim,
> 1897:648)

In this chapter, we will compare some of the features of
social organization of the "cult of man" movements, first to
corresponding features of the Catholic Charismatic Renewal
movement (CCR) which locates the sacred outside the individual,
and secondly, the turn-of-the-century Canadian cults, whose
view of the sacred is akin to the "cult of man" groups.

I The "Cult of Man" and the Catholic Charismatic Renewal Movement[2]

Working from the most apparent and exterior forms of
such social organization, we may detect four obvious contrasts
between the organization of the Charismatics and the
organization of the "cult of man" groups. These are:
(a) charismatic community vs. fee-for-service coursework;
(b) community vs. individual development; (c) permanence vs.
transience; (d) total vs. partial commitment. It will be
argued in this chapter that not only do these four features
of "cult of man" groups distinguish them from a group like
the Catholic Charismatics, but may be used to make the finer
distinction between the harmonial groups, occult and healing,
of the turn-of-the-century, and the contemporary "cult of
man." In this latter instance, the differences are questions
of degree, but they are still present.

A. Charismatic Community vs. Fee-
   For-Service Coursework

One of the things which is unique about the "cult of man"
groups is their high-price coursework format. With the
exception of yoga groups (who charge a minimal fee for
lessons) no other new religious movements follow this
procedure. There are two elements involved in this contrast:
the exchange of 'fees' and the coursework structure. We will
examine each of these in turn as compared to the Catholic
Charismatic Renewal movement.

1. Fees vs. Voluntary Contributions

It is interesting to examine the implications of charging
fees as opposed to financing through voluntary contributions.
While all religious groups in order to survive must develop
methods to help support themselves, this has rarely in the
past been done by demanding money as a criterion for
participation as opposed to a responsibility of those who
have already committed themselves. While some branches of
the Charismatics, housed in the buildings of the Catholic
churches and led by priests employed by that Catholic church,
do not have any overhead and therefore do not have even ritual
collection, for those with expenses this is usually the means
for insuring funds. For other new religious movements, such
as the monastic wing of the Zen Buddhists, the Dharma Datu,
the Sri Chinmoy, which locate in a communal centre, financing
is often on the basis of a cut of the salary of the individual
members. Groups such as the Hare Krishna or the Unification
Church, whose members remove themselves totally from the
general occupational structure, find support through
soliciting funds or through group-run work projects such as
selling flowers, or opening a restaurant.

These methods of collecting money seem haphazard and
unreliable compared to the fee-for-service method of the
"cult of man." Est charges $300 for two weekends per person,
Arica charges between $75 for an introductory weekend, and
$1500 for a 40 day workshop (cost for courses in Arica varies
somewhat depending on the location). Silva Mind Control asks
$150 for a week (five evenings and a weekend), Psychosynthesis
charges approximately $150 for ten evening group sessions.
In that way the organization seems to insure its support,

whether or not members become committed in the long run. This seems like a sensible solution to the dilemma of financing.

However, as Weber (1925) has documented, the relationship between religion and finance is an uneasy one at best. He argues that it is the need for economic subsistence which is one of the major features in the routinization process whereby the Charismatic sect, with the intense, direct religious experience it offers, becomes compromised. Money is "the most impersonal and abstract element that exists in human life," Weber argues (Gerth and Mills, 1958:331). It depersonalizes any relationship it enters into. For this reason, religion (particularly the salvation religion of North American society, grounded as it is in the ethic of brotherly love) has tended to shun the whole world of economics, seeing money as dirty and evil. Dealings with money are dangerous, and must be carried out with great care in order to avoid the contamination of the sacred. The solutions have been reliance on charity (as in Indian Buddhism where itinerant monks are supported by the lay population who give their money as a substitute for their participation) (Weber, 1958) or donations by members of some part of their income, either in a voluntary or ritualistic way. In either of these latter two cases, such a giving is part of the commitment process, a way in which the adherent pledges his worldly activity as at the service of the sacred and hence, to some extent, sanctifies it.

On the other hand, the "cult of man" would appear to have compromised and endangered the sacred from the moment of initiation. The sacred is 'bought'; the relationship to the leader-teacher depersonalized. We will see in the next chapter how this sort of relationship between religion and finance is only possible with the concept of the sacred held by these groups. However, for the moment, we will turn to that element of group organization linked intimately to the mode of finance: the coursework structure.

2. The Coursework Format vs. the Charismatic Community

Both the fee-for-service and the coursework format are elements of what Weber would term 'rationalization'. Rationalization is identified with bureaucracy, rational efficiency, continuity of operation, speed, precision and calculation of results (in short, all those aspects of modern society which counter-cultural theorists have seen adherents of new religious movements as reacting against). Yet, rationalization of this nature has always been seen as foreign to religion, particularly to emerging cults or sects which places emphasis on the mystical, the ecstatic, the direct experience of the irrational (Gerth and Mills, 1958:331-333). The "cult of man" offers a paradoxical picture in this respect. In some ways it fits with Weber's description of charismatic cults. While the relationship between teacher and trainee is a depersonalized one in some respects, and the student is seen as buying a knowledge that will make him the equal of the instructor, the founders of such movements, such as José Silva, Werner Erhard, Oscar Ichazo, Robert Assogioli, L. Ron Hubbard, E. J. Gold, are mysterious and undoubtedly charismatic figures. What's more, in the individual class the lack of hierarchy, the sense of equality and sense of being virtuosi are all features which associate "cult of man" groups with charasmatic cults (Weber, 1925). But the rational coursework format and the fees are crucial differences.

Much more common in the history of new religious movements and among contemporary movements are the Catholic Charismatics who see themselves not as a class but as a community, joined not by their desire to know but by their special knowledge. Their 'gifts' are intrinsic, not to be bought ... their group leaders (particularly in Montreal, where most groups are led by priests) are seen as having "all the gifts."

The coursework vs. community organization has other implications. In groups such as Arica, est, Silva Mind Control and Scientology, members sit in chairs facing the instructor; in the CCR meetings, members sit in a circle facing each other. While the CCR group has a seminar of the Spirit, in which the scriptures are described and discussed, the "cult of man" groups give preset classes defined by training manuals. While at the end of the seminars of the spirit members may receive the Baptism of the Spirit, an intensely emotional and mystical experience, the 'graduate' of a class from the "cult of man" receives (in some cases

after an examination) a 'certificate'. While for the
Charismatic, the Baptism of the Spirit marks his entrance, in
one step, into the community, the certificate marks for the
"cult of man" member, his release back into the world, the
dissolution of the group, unless he wants to pay another fee
and take a course at a higher level, which these groups
(notably Psychosynthesis, Scientology) offer. This latter
point brings us to the next organizational feature which
distinguishes "cult of man" groups: its inherent transience
vs. the permanency offered by the CCR and other such groups.

B. Transience vs. Permanence

One of the most central features of the "cult of man"
groups is their emphasis on change and on transience.
Certainly in each case there are instructors whose participation is continual over time, or at least does not have a
definite termination date. However, for the majority who
would consider themselves adherents of these movements, the
group life is formally restricted.

A group like Shakti makes nearly a fetish out of the
concept of planned obsolescence. This group periodically
shuts down its centres, sends away their students unexpectedly,
sometimes in mid-course, and changes its organizational name.

> These carefully planned, highly ritualized "turn offs"
> can be interpreted as the final lesson of the course.
> One of the "ruts" the group is attacking is of course
> preconditioned ideas of what constitutes a religious
> movement and a spiritual master ... stranding students
> can be seen as a way to make them change themselves,
> change society and not become a comfortable member of
> a clique. (Palmer, 1976:101-102)

Even in a group like Psychosynthesis, where the interaction during group meetings is intense, and a series of
advancement courses are offered which allow adherents a
continual link to the institute over some time, each 'group'
composed of a class of people dissolves after the last
meeting. Adherents may feel a sense of loss about this, but
in general, this is seen as a part of the growth experience.
For instance, note the following interchange which took place
at the last group meeting of a Psychosynthesis group:

> Lisa: It makes me sad ... I feel like I'd like to
>   pack everyone a lunch to take with them.

> John: I think that what we're feeling is the group ending which is like a death.
>
> Laurie: I don't feel sad at all, I don't feel like its a death. I feel really good about it ... I've really gotten something out of the group.
>
> Alice (group leader): Well, every end is a little bit like a death but it is also a beginning. We all have lives outside that we go on with. Its good to go on ... but its also good to recognize the sadness, to take responsibility for that feeling ... unless we recognize it, it's like the ghosts of other members (of the group) just keep hanging around our lives, getting in the way ... this way we say good-bye and send them on their way ...
>
>   - Psychosynthesis group meeting

In this sense "cult of man" groups are historical experiences, occupying a finite period of time. The group dissolves and the individuals carry on.

Contrast this with the groups such as the CCR in which the group is seen as having a life which transcends the individual members. Members come and go, live and die, but the body of the group remains. It is interesting to compare the reactions of members of the Psychosynthesis group noted above with those of a small CCR group who have been told they ought to merge with a larger CCR group. Despite the fact that the larger group was one all members knew, and indeed sometimes attended, they clung to the smaller group.

> Father N: Father K. says that sometimes there is a lot of tension in small groups.
>
> Leila: But when the Holy Spirit first came to the disciples, they were only a small group, they were only eleven and he came to them ...
>
> Father N: But I feel that if the pastor is against a prayer meeting it shouldn't be held.
>
> Joan: To heck with the pastor. We've got the room, we'll just lock the door and have our prayer meeting (much laughter and protestations). I think we've put a lot of effort into these prayer meetings. We're like one family now. We can't just give it up.
>
>   - CCR group meeting

To dissolve the group seemed unthinkable, like dissolving a family who were all connected by blood. For the

Psychosynthesis members and those of other "cult of man" groups, such a dissolution was seen as desirable, a part of individual growth.

Other structural aspects of group life also support this contrast between transience and permanence. The meetings of the CCR follow a cyclical pattern, once a week prayer meetings, once a week mass, at the same time every week. In addition, the CCR members participate in the yearly cycle of Christian rituals. The meetings of the "cult of man" groups is not cyclical, but progressive moving from beginning to end, from introduction to conclusion in a linear continuum. Finally, the location of group meetings also emphasizes this contrast. The "cult of man" groups meet in secular and temporary locations such as a rented hall, or a hotel conference room. The CCR groups meet in a fixed spot, a centre, and often a room in the local parish church, which they decorate with pennants and other emblems to mark out the space as their own.

This contrast between transience on the one hand, and permanence on the other, is closely connected to the third distinction: that between community development and individual development.

C.   Community Development vs. Individual Development

As in this chapter we are concerned not with the belief system of these groups but in the contrast between types of social organization, we will discuss the above dichotomy in organizational terms. This contrast is closely connected to the notion we mentioned in the previous section, i.e. that for the "cult of man" groups, the community is seen as transient, whereas in the CCR (and related groups) it is the individual who is seen as transient. This has profound implications for the type of interaction which goes on between members at group meetings.

In the "cult of man" groups, this interaction is minimal. At the extreme of a group like est, no interaction is set up or organized. Individuals do stand up to use a microphone to testify to the changes which have occurred in their lives or in their minds. The other students react to this as an audience, by cheering. In contrast groups such as the

Charismatics, a testimonial about the changes in a person's
life are met with by enthusiasm and involvement, encouraged by
the community as a means by which members become really part
of the group, "become charismatic" (Westley, 1977). Even a
group such as Psychosynthesis, which, as we have noted,
encourages interaction, discourages involvement which would
forge the members into a group. Contrast the two interactions
below, the first having taken place in a Charismatic group
meeting, the second in a Psychosynthesis group meeting.

a) Gary: Before everyone goes ... I'd like ... I
don't need to be prayed over, but maybe
we could say a prayer ... I'm taking
swimming lessons and I'm scared of the
water ... I'd have to go in the deep end
this week ... Maybe everyone could pray
so I won't be afraid.

Barbara: Why don't you want us to pray over you?

Gary: It doesn't seem important enough.

Barbara: Of course its important enough. Come on
everybody. (We pray over Gary).

- CCR group meeting

b) John: I feel sad to think this group is ending.
I really enjoyed this kind of encounter.
I wonder why in real life people don't
communicate the way we do here. If I try
to talk to people at work about the
higher self people look at me like I'm
crazy.

Jim: It seems to me that if you just act the
way you want to, then even if some people
don't like you others will ... you may
find some sympathetic souls out there.

Alice: (group leader): Jim, I'm hearing you
trying to tell John what to do, and I'm
hearing John just wanting to be sad, not
wanting to do anything with it. Is there
something hooking you here?

- Psychosynthesis group meeting

In the first instance, a member brings a difficulty from
his personal life which is used by members as a way of
involving themselves with him, bringing them closer. They
pray for him and will continue to do so (and inquire how the
swimming lessons are going) for weeks. In the second instance,
a difficulty on the part of a member is met with advice from
another member, advice which is questioned by the group leader

as insensitivity and over-identification (to be hooked is to confuse self with the other). The advising member is told to leave the first member to experience his sadness.

Another example of the difference between these two groups is the sense of responsibility which they feel for each other. When one member of the CCR sprained her ankle leaving the meeting, three other members went home with her and stayed a good part of the night. In contrast after each meeting, members of the Psychosynthesis group dispersed individually. The watchword in this group was that members should "take responsibility for their own actions." A party organized for the week after classes ended was attended by only a third of participants. It should be stressed again that of all the "cult of man" groups, Psychosynthesis encourages the most interaction among members. In est, entering students are counselled that they must not sit next to anyone that they know.

D. Partial vs. Total Involvement

The preceding opposition served as an indicator of the general nature of interaction within these two types of groups. This opposition provides a measure of the intensity of such interaction. As noted earlier, members of groups such as the Charismatics, gather at least twice a week for their prayer meetings and the regular Sunday mass. In addition, particularly in larger groups, individual 'ministries' will meet other nights of the week. Special dinners for couples will involve spouses who are not members of the Charismatics. In Ann Arbor, where the movement is centred, there are a number of communal living units for members of the Charismatics (Keene, 1974). This is not unusual for this type of Christian revival movement, or for such eastern imports which clearly locate the sacred as outside the individual such as the Unification Church, the Hare Krishna and Sri Chinmoy. Members of the "cult of man" groups, however, do not live together in centres. They may encourage their children or spouses to take the course (est is particularly renowned for this) but for the most part, the course, like all courses, is an experience which the individual compartmentalizes from the rest of his life.

Members may use what they learned in their regular lives, but they take their knowledge out to the world, whereas members of the Charismatics, to the extent that they continue participation in the world, tend to bring the world into the meeting, interpreting and reinterpreting the events of their lives in terms of the truths of the group (Westley, 1977:931).

The initiation ritual is a nice point of comparison. As we noted, for the "cult of man" members it involves a payment of a fee and the reception of a certificate, both 'impersonal' acts in Weber's terms. The initiation for the Charismatics is the Baptism of the Holy Spirit, a highly emotional moment, when group members cluster around the initiate, place their hands on his or her head and pray over him/her, and the member often receives the gift of tongues, or reacts with tears, to a sense of the 'inrushing of the spirit' from which experience the initiate emerges transformed, a new person (Gerlach and Hines, 1970). It is worth noting in this connection that when members of such groups as Silva Mind Control were asked the question, "could you describe your present involvement with this group?" they answered uniformly that they were instructors, or had 'taken the course' or practiced a certain technique regularly. Members of the Catholic Charismatics asked such a question, responded in a manner such as follows:

> It is a very integral part of my life.
> It is the high point of my week. It is where I go to
> get my batteries recharged. I experience a deeper
> sense of peace there than anywhere else. It is
> being fulfilled ...
>
> — CCR members

Participation for the "cult of man" member is defined in terms of an action or actions and a role. For the Charismatic the experience is considerably more holistic, involving the identity and life experience of the member. This is not to say that members of a "cult of man" group will not claim that the experience changed their occupations, friends, performance on the job, health, methods of handling problems or approaching people. But these changes are always couched in terms of self-transformation, they do not express the identity shift and community commitment expressed by the Charismatics.

This difference in the degree of involvement is underlined by the fact that most "cult of man" members are
eclectic. They see many different paths to truth. They may
have tried other new religious movements (yoga groups seem to
be the favourite) and they may maintain an identification
with another, mainstream religion. They don't see other
groups as 'evil' or 'dangerous' although they may have their
personal preferences. However, the Charismatics clearly see
other groups as dangerous. One Charismatic Renewal member
confided that the priest who led the biggest group in Montreal
saw TM members as possessed and in need of exorcism.

II   The Cult-Sect Dichotomy: The "Cult of Man"
      and Harmonial Cults

To this point in this chapter, we have noted that the
"cult of man" groups in contemporary America differ from
groups that clearly hold the sacred as lying outside the
individual in at least four respects. In terms of their
social organization, these groups emphasize a rational coursework structure, and a fee-type financial system, as opposed to
a charity or donation system and worship service format.
Secondly, they are finite groups, emphasizing the transience
of community as opposed to the permanence of community
stressed by the Charismatics. Thirdly, they emphasize
individual development as opposed to community development
and, fourthly, ask, indeed demand, only partial commitment of
members as opposed to total commitment. Do these differences
indicate that the "cult of man" groups are indeed something
new in the history of religious movements, peculiar to the
highly specialized, diversified and technological society, as
Durkheim would have predicted?

One of the problems in answering this question is the
fact that the differences that we have outlined for our
particular case correspond to some of the classic differences
between 'cult' and 'sect' which theorists in sociology of
religion, since Troeltsch, have recognized as distinct types
of religious organization. Cults have been variously
described as having an organization which is shortlived, very
loose, much more compromised in financial and ideal terms
with the dominant society than sects, with a much greater
emphasis on the individual as opposed to the community

(Yinger, 1951; Ellwood, 1973; Troeltsch, 1931; Mann, 1972).
In addition, however, cults have been in existence, at
different historical moments, since early Greek and Roman
times (in short, as far back as there is extensive
documentation of religious life). Granted, it has been noted
(Ellwood, 1973; Mann, 1972) that cults have an elective
affinity with cosmopolitan cultures and urban environments,
seeming to reflect the fluid, diversified and pluralistic
components always found in the social organization of such
societies. If, however, the organization of the "cult of
man" is no different from cults throughout time, then the
kind of religious evolution which Durkheim predicted would be
specific to the increasing differentiation of our society,
cannot be said to be reflected in the "cult of man."

The fact that cults per se tend to appear in cosmopolitan
and urban societies, supports Durkheim's basic hypothesis
about the relationship between religious and social organization. However, just as the elements of pluralism,
diversification and specialization present, to some degree,
in all urban, cosmopolitan societies, have been developed and
extended to an unprecedented extent in 20th century North
American society, so if Durkheim is correct we would expect
to find in contemporary religion not only more cults but
shifts in cult organization in the direction of becoming more
extreme, more compromised financially and ideally, more
individualistic, shorter lived than cults at other times.

While we do not have the data to investigate the first
prediction that more cults (proportionately) exist now than
in previous periods, we may determine if there has been a
shift in the social organization of cults over time. While
this point could be proved by comparing modern cults to early
gnostic cults of the second century, it is even better proved
by comparing them to groups designated as cults in turn-of-
the-century America. These have the advantage of sharing the
cultural milieu of North America, as well as some of the basic
ideological orientations with the "cult of man" groups. As it
happens, there is also particularly good data on Canadian
chapters of such cults documented in Mann (1972) which help to
render the comparison specific. If it is possible to document
that there has been a shift in cult organization in the

direction of increased rationalization, individualism, transience and partial involvement, this would suggest support for the idea that cult organization has been sensitive to the shift in social organization towards greater diversity, specialization, pluralism elements, which Durkheim predicted would be responsible for the "cult of man."

In Mann's comparative study of cult, sect and church in Alberta, he analyses data collected on ten cults. The first five, Christian Science, Unity, Church of Truth, Divine Science, Spiritualism, he terms 'healing' or 'metaphysical' groups, the second five, the Rosicrucians, Theosopy, Church of New Jerusalem, I am, Consumer's Movement, he terms 'occult, esoteric or mystical'.

Healing and occult cults varied somewhat in terms of doctrine according to Mann, but shared a number of organizational features. The cultists formed a kind of sub-culture in Calgary society. People moved easily from one type of cult to another (a fact which caused Mann to term this element of the membership 'metaphysical tramps') although this movement generally followed a pattern from healing to occult groups and members were well known to each other. Membership in these cults was in many cases not recorded at all. The most that was expected seemed to be signing a membership card (Mann, 1972:80). Mann notes that the cults in Alberta made much greater compromises with the secular environment than did the sects. This was manifest both in the practical things such as wealth and happiness which members were encouraged to seek from God, and by the methods of evangelism used ... depending largely on highly rationalized business and advertisement techniques (Ibid.: 142). Mann also notes that the local leaders of most groups had a very great deal of influence and power.

While many, if not all of these characteristics are shared by "cult of man" groups and cults in general, some important differences in organization may be revealed by a comparison of the following two accounts of group meetings in (a) a New Thought group, and (b) a Silva Mind Control group.

> a) While the group was getting seated, an elderly
> woman played a bit of Tschaikowsky, and after
> Miss Chew (the leader) took her place on the

platform, the group sang two hymns, "Rock of
Ages, Truth Divine" and "Sweet Hour of Prayer."
Miss Chew began with announcements; she said
that she would have office hours daily between
two and five p.m. There was to be a meeting
the next night to discuss a new location for
the church, since she (Miss Chew) was being
evicted ... After the announcements the group
repeated "I rejoice in the power of Good,"
twice. Miss Chew requested that people turn in
their vacation envelopes because during the past
month the church's income had ceased. (This was
a service in late August). The group then said
'Divine love' three times and the offering was
taken. A great many one and five dollar bills
appeared on the plate. Miss Chew announced that
she had just returned from the International New
Thought Highlights conference. Among the
speakers in Milwaukee was Ernest Wilson, editor
of the Los Angeles magazine called <u>Progress for
Unity</u>. She said that he was a small, sunburned,
genial man with a winning smile ... another
speaker at the conference was Louise Newman, who
said, "Its great to be human! Every person
should have an ideal and climb up to it.
Identify yourself with the inner mind of God and
keep saying I know and I know that I know. You
can't press clothes with a cold iron; there must
be a contact with power to be effective."
Dr. Myers, another speaker, said that people
think that all they have to do is look at Christ
and they will be healed forever. Actually the
power is within us and God in embryo is within
each of us. Therefore, we should refrain from
setting up negative inner forces ... Dr. Gregg
of Toronto told the conference that healing is
our birthright. Look for harmony and you will
find health, an inner harmony everywhere. It
is easier to say the word "well" than the word
"sickness." It is important to remember that
our aim is to "get heaven into men rather than
to get men into heaven." Miss Chew ended the
service with a prayer that asked for the
opportunity to leave an imprint on those who
follow us. The knowledge of God dwells within
us, let us use it correctly. The congregation
sang "I See Abundance Everywhere" and Miss Chew
said in closing, "no vision is too great for
you. Live at peace."
    Miss Chew was an elderly woman with well-
groomed white hair. She wore a pale blue evening
gown and a corsage of roses was pinned to her
dress. She spoke quietly without emotion. She
seemed to be talking to a group of friends. Her
speech was fluent and her vocabulary and grammar
were good. She was neither intense nor emotional,
just calm and quiet. The atmosphere was relaxed
and peaceful as a result of her personality.

(Mann, 1972:59)

b) As the Silva Mind Control courses were carried on over a week, each evening was different. They followed, however, a predictable pattern. The following is an example:

> The meeting began with a talk by the leader about "mental housecleaning," the importance of positive thought and the use of the phrase 'cancel cancel' to block out negative thoughts. Secondly, the leader talked about the unused potential of the human brain. "We can function as psychics. How or why we aren't concerned with ... we're not concerned with the mechanism. What matters is that effects can be felt and used." He continued to argue that knowing about the potential but not using it is "in the religious sense the largest sin." We are under moral obligation to use it.
>
> After this lecture there was a question period. People asked questions about why the brain 'levels' on the chart (at the front of the room) were 'colour coded' and were told the colours weren't significant. Someone else said that they felt a kind of fear about "going to deeper levels" and was that normal, and how 'far' should she go. She was told, "As far as you want ... it's your mind." If frightening images come she was told to change them with "psychic surgery." The leader added that we were all likely as we got more 'into' our minds, to have startlingly clear images of people and things. "We are opening our-selves up to lots of psychic and spiritual impulses floating around."
>
> After the question session we did three con-ditionings. People assumed a relaxed position, eyes closed, and the instructor read the instructions verbatim from a manual. The conditioning was for going to sleep on command, waking up on command and remembering dreams. In each case the conditioning involved relaxing "going down to level" and then mentally repeating the formula, which the instructor read out.
>
> After the last conditioning, the meeting broke up. One of the other leaders told a small group the story of having her baby by C-section without anaesthetic, just using mind control to kill the pain.

It may be noted immediately that these two cults differ in their degree of rationalization. The "New Thought" cult employs non-rational (in Weberian terms) means of financing by collection, while the SMC group charges fees. Secondly, while New Thought, when compared to sectarian groups, seems to appeal on rational and intellectual terms as opposed to emotional, it is not rational in the sense of being bureaucratic, efficient, methodical or standardized. On the contrary, the meetings are kept informal by avoiding set routine. In contrast, SMC meetings follow a pre-programmed order, following detailed written instructions. The only informal or spontaneous aspects were the question and answer periods that came after each 'formula type technique' was taught and during the two coffee breaks which took place each evening.

It may be argued that what we see elements of in the New Thought lecture format have been developed and refined to a much greater degree in a group like Silva Mind Control. This latter group not only uses business and advertising techniques in proselytizing, but its very meetings are pre-programmed, unvarying, and formal, to a degree equalled only by the most routinized 'church' setting.

It can, therefore, be argued that on the rational-charismatic continuum separating sects and cults traditionally, contemporary cults have become even more consistently rational than those which emerged in the early part of this century.

A similar development is evident in terms of the transience-permanence continuum. While, in fact, as Mann notes, a group like New Thought and the cults of the turn-of-the-century were of _indeterminate_ and usually short life, they were not, on the other hand, of _finite_ and short life. Their membership simply never grew, and no effort was made to keep track of those who left. They also depended, as we have pointed out, on a rather shaky financial basis. Nevertheless, while in existence they tended to have a stable centre or church, and perhaps more importantly, a 'round' of activities including Sunday service and at least one mid-weekly meeting. Hence, the members themselves were not aware of a definite termination date for group life. Meetings provided a continual weekly structure which, at least as far as they knew (since obsolescence wasn't planned) might continue indefinitely. Therefore, while the cults of the turn-of-the-century were undoubtedly much more transient in character than were the sects of the same period, they were not yet formally transient experiences like contemporary "cult of man" groups. Once again along this important dimension, we find that the development has been towards more extreme 'cultic' behavior.

There remain two other dimensions, total vs. partial involvement and community vs. individual development. Along these two dimensions the difference between "cult of man" groups and turn-of-the-century cults is not as pronounced. Some distinctions do, however, remain. For example, Mann has pointed out the importance of the local leader for most cults. In the above description of the meeting, the leader speaks to the members in a friendly motherly fashion. While such links may not give the community the kind of cohesion found in sects, it, nevertheless, ties members together in a common focus: their relationship to the leader. In contrast, while members of "cult of man" groups may hold the national leader (Erhard, Silva, Ichazo) in considerable reverence, the majority never meet this leader. Their major contact with the cult is with the individual instructor. These are seldom invested with the kind of charisma that the national leader is invested with, or, for that matter, that the local leader of the turn-of-the-century cults exercised over his/her followers. Once again, the financial dimension enters in here. The instructor is paid in the "cult of man." He provides the student with a skill. Once the student has mastered this skill, he is potentially the equal of the instructor. For example, at the end of each section of the Silva Mind Control course, the student is provided with a pamphlet-manual containing the exact words and instructions which the leader used in guiding the student through the exercise the first time. The student is from then on able to be his or her own instructor. Hence, it might be argued that while the turn-of-the-century cults had no more interaction between members than "cult of man" groups, they had considerably more leader-follower interaction and interdependence. This, in turn, provided a potential bond between members not present in the "cult of man." At least in this respect the turn-of-the-century cults put more emphasis on community development than do "cult of man" groups.

In a separate but related manner the actual interaction at group meetings also suggests more community emphasis in turn-of-the-century cults. For instance, note that in the New Thought meetings the group sing hymns together, repeat affirmations ('Divine Love') together and listen to the sermon/lecture together. Silva Mind Control members also repeat affirmations but they do so silently and to themselves rather than with the group. In both cases, these affirmations, prayers, etc. may be for selfish and individualistic ends and so fail to overtly develop a sense of community. But the New Thought members at least continue to share an outward focus as they verbalize their affirmations and sing hymns together. The focus of ritual action in the Silva Mind Control group is inward. Whether or not the member performs the ritual or in what manner is known only to himself. In this aspect as well, it would seem that the turn-of-the-century cults, while being individualistic, were not as extreme as the "cult of man" groups today.

Lastly, there is the question of total vs. partial involvement in the movement. The fluidity with which Mann noted that members came and left, and with which groups formed and dissolved in Calgary, certainly suggests that the commit-ment to the groups was far from total. Also, the emphasis on taking the power tapped in the movement out to the world instead of bringing the world into the group seems very similar to the attitude we noted in contemporary "cult of man" groups. However, there is one factor which seems to argue to the contrary, and that is the composition of the membership. Mann has noted that members, while they tended to be middle class and of comfortable income, were, nevertheless, in some ways socially marginal, "poorly integrated into the community" (Mann, 1972:42). They were disproportionately single or widowed middle-aged women (the ratio of women to men was 6:1). They also tended toward excessive residential mobility. The leaders of these movements, both local and national, were also disproportionately women. What this suggests is that members led rather empty, lonely lives devoid even of the driving edge of financial difficulty. It can be hypothesized that for such women a cult would become a much more central experience with fewer competing commitments or activities to challenge the member's loyalty or (at least temporary) involvement. In contrast, the membership of the "cult of man" today is younger, equally divided between men and women (with a slight predominance of men in some groups) and have leaders who are disproportionately male (Stone, 1976; Tipton, 1977; Wuthnow,

1976a). For the most part, then, these are individuals who
have competing time and loyalty commitments, if not to their
families ("cult of man" groups have a large percentage of
single, residentially mobile members as well) then at least in
terms of their occupations. The distinction is slight and
largely inductive.[3] It is certainly along this dimension of
partial vs. total commitment that turn-of-the-century and
"cult of man" groups seem to have most in common. However,
the distinction is present, however slight and once again, it
would seem to be the contemporary "cult of man" groups which
focus most on individual development and least on total
participation.

In sum, by comparing superficial organizational factors
of turn-of-the-century cults and contemporary "cult of man"
groups, it would appear that they do share a general "cult"
orientation of being rationalized, short-lived,
individualistic and pluralistic when compared to sects of the
present or of the past. However, on each of these dimensions
the "cult of man" groups seem to be more extreme than the
cults of the turn-of-the-century. This would seem to lend
support to the notion that the cult in general is a religious
form particularly sensitive to and expressive of technological
society, and that as the fluidity, diversity and
specialization of the latter becomes more pronounced, so do
the corresponding elements of cult organization. Mann himself
suggested such an affinity, stressing that therein lay the
significance of the cults in his study:

> Cultism thus in Alberta reflected in accentuated
> form the instabilities of urban society. In this way
> it probably had a social significance much greater
> than would seem indicated by the small numbers
> attached to it. Its appeal to people apparently well
> educated and reasonably well off economically suggest
> that in certain large areas of our urban society --
> among that section of the population conventionally
> thought of as the staid middle class -- exist trouble
> spots only yet slightly explored. (Mann, 1972:158)

In the next chapter we will move from a discussion of
the social organization of the "cult of man" to the belief
system. If Durkheim is correct, it will be argued that not
only should the extreme differences in organization that
exist between the "cult of man" groups and a sectarian group

like the Catholic Charismatic Renewal movement be reflected in extremely different beliefs, but the subtle differences in cult organization discussed above should be apparent in subtly different beliefs held by cults at these two different historical moments.

CHAPTER VI

DISTINGUISHING BELIEFS OF THE "CULT OF MAN": A COMPARATIVE VIEW

In this chapter we will turn from an examination of the social structure of new religious movements to a comparison of the beliefs held by these movements. As noted, our original selection of the "cult of man" groups was based on the conception of the sacred held by such groups: the "cult of man" groups all locate the sacred within, as opposed to outside of, the individual. We noted in the last chapter that groups having this conception of the sacred differed from those groups which located the sacred outside the individual along four important organizational dimensions. In this chapter we will examine the belief systems of the "cult of man" in slightly more detail, focusing in particular upon those elements of belief which seem to correspond to, or flow from, the distinctive elements of social structure which we examined in the last chapter.

Once again, as a control, we will compare these beliefs to the belief systems of (a) the CCR movement, which contrasts with the "cult of man" groups on all social structure dimensions, and (b) with turn-of-the-century cults which, while sharing with the "cult of man" groups some elements basic to 'cult' organization, are considerably less extreme in many of their features.

The argument in this chapter is as follows: if Durkheim is correct in his basic hypotheses about the relationship of belief and social structure, we would expect to find differences in the beliefs of "cult of man" and CCR groups that correspond to the already documented differences in social organization. When comparing "cult of man" groups to turn-of-the-century cults, we would expect their beliefs to be similar to the "cult of man," although less extreme.

To summarize in advance, it will be suggested in this chapter that corresponding to the economic/organizational rationality of the "cult of man" groups, there exists a belief in the efficacy of the techniques, tools and terms of

59

science. This attitude towards science may be seen to
represent an advance in conceptual rationality over turn-of-
the-century groups to match the increase in structural
rationality. Secondly, the contrast between community and
individual development on the organizational level is
reflected in a corresponding contrast between a belief in
healing and a belief in purity. Finally, it is suggested
that two contrasts, that between transience and permanence,
and that between individual and partial involvement on the
organization level, are reflected in a contrast between a
belief in the internal unity of the individual adherent and
a sense of internal fragmentation. The rationales for these
analogies between structural and conceptual oppositions will
be explained individually.

Faith vs. Scientific Technology

The tension between religion and science has been discussed to the point where it has become a cliché. At the
root of this tension is seen to be a conflict similar to that
between economics and religion; the one drives toward
rationalization, efficiency and predictability in the material
world, the other sees the irrational and the unpredictable as
essential aspects of the supernatural, which for religion
forms the basis for all reality, natural or supernatural.

In our discussion of new religious movements, we are
interested in several different aspects of science. We are
first interested in the group's attitude toward the
scientific perspective, i.e. the general approach of science
to discovering and interpreting reality.

Secondly, we are interested in the attitude of new
religious movements to scientific language, techniques and
tools. If our predictions are correct, therefore, we would
expect "cult of man" groups to make greater use of scientific
perspectives, language, techniques and explanations than the
CCR and to use them differently than the turn-of-the-century
cults. In this latter exploration, we are interested in this
section (and in the subsequent chapter on the rituals which
flow from these beliefs and attitudes) in exploring the
particular nature of the "cult of man's" relationship to
science, which makes it different from that of

turn-of-the-century groups.

The threat science has always posed to religion lies in its meaning system. Science provides an alternate interpretation of the world and many of its historical elements, which directly contradict those suggested by religion. Further, it suggests that the world works by laws comprehensible, not incomprehensible, to man. It sees Man as the Actor as opposed to the Reactor. It therefore poses a threat to the reality of the sacred, the mystical, which by definition, is unpredictable and incomprehensible.

Most new religious movements, like the CCR group, come to terms with science by compartmentalizing the two, and/or by ranking scientific language, explanations and techniques as hierarchically inferior to religious. Hence, a CCR member, if ill, will certainly see a doctor and receive what treatment is available. On the other hand, other members will pray for the ill person, and the general consensus is that whether the person lives or dies is not finally dependent on the doctor, but on the decision of God. Other issues, such as scientific ethics (euthanasia, for instance) are generally ignored, as "not being our concern."

The Charismatics on the whole, however, are significantly devoid of scientific perspectives, language, techniques and explanations. They generally seem to ignore social science as well, although they are extremely suspicious of field workers. In one group, many members suggested to the field worker that she might be possessed by the devil; in another, members balked at the term "interview," stating things like, "I don't give interviews, I just praise the Lord." The two (interview and the Lord) were somehow seen to be in opposition.

Hence, the attitude toward science and social science in the CCR movement is to some degree one of avoidance. This attitude contrasts markedly with that of members of "cult of man" groups who are quite open to researchers, although they are seen occasionally as misguided:

> When I announced my intention of writing a paper on them, they were amused and decided to mislead and confuse me, sending me off on wild goose chases and false scents, with the intention of undermining my academic stance in the hope that I would eventually

> see the futility of trying to explain a spiritual
> phenomenum in rational terms. (Palmer, 1976:4)

The "cult of man" groups are replete with scientific and
social scientific explanations, terminology and techniques.
In many cases, copies of scientific experiments which indicate
the positive physical effects of meditation or alpha brain
waves are handed out in the first class. Terminology from
information theory and computor science (such as cancel,
encode, decode, data, program) are used extensively to deal
with human communication and thought processes by groups like
Shakti, Scientology and SMC. Shakti calls itself "The
Spiritual Science of DNA," Aricans talk about the human brain
as a meta-computor. Psychosynthesis draws heavily on
psychological and sociological terminology talking about norms
and projections. Lastly, some actual tools such as biofeedback machines, lie detector machines, and EEC recordings,
which have been shown to be useful instruments in scientific
experiments, are used in these groups for unscientific ends.

However, despite the borrowing of terminology, tool,
technique and even explanation, "cult of man" groups reject
rational thought and the scientific perspective. Like the
CCR, they value experience, not rational knowledge. They
indeed find systematic explanations an anathema, alien to the
sacred:

> Go easy on the explanations without demonstrations ...
> no matter what the student says about how they under-
> stand ... while a personality can learn to appreciate
> and store up information intellectually, we want to
> teach something to the Being, and the Being can learn
> only by experience. There isn't any intellect there.
> No mind there. (Gold, 1973:68)

This apparent inconsistency between perspective and
technique is better understood by examining the methods for
achieving experience in a given "cult of man" group. Take,
for example, the methods used by SMC for attaining psychic
experiences.

The entering student into the SMC course finds at the
front of the classroom (where the altar stands in many turn-
of-the-century cults and contemporary sects) a chart of the
brain levels. It is explained to the student that "through
the use of the sensitive amplifier used to record brain

frequencies, the EEG, or electroencephalogram, four basic
types of impulses have been classified" (SMC handout). These
four types include beta, associated with sense perception,
alpha, associated with daydreaming, theta, associated with
sleep (and it is hinted, creativity) and delta, associated
with deep sleep and the state of newborn infants.

These brain waves have indeed been recognized by science.
They are scientific _fact_ as is their association with certain
mental activity. However, the causal connections have not
been firmly established.

SMC doctrine, however, seizes these facts and then proceeds to build a fantastic edifice with these few blocks.
For one thing, the brain wave frequencies are visualized
spatially, not as points on a continuum, but as levels in an
internal building, delta being the "deepest" level. These
"levels" are given a physiological reality by SMC identification of the "delta" as the "oldest portion" of the brain (the
back) and "alpha" and "beta" more recent and front levels.
These older levels are also seen as "healthier." This is a
belief translated from the occult ... that there exists
"ancient wisdom" that if we may recapture will yield great
power.

Having, by a sort of poetic license with the term
"level," created internal spaces to coincide with brain wave
frequencies, these then become worlds which the adherents can
reach through a series of techniques, _also borrowed from_
scientific experiment (biofeedback in particular) to induce
relaxation. Adherents are told through a simple count-down
method (no measurement by instruments is done to determine
when or if slower frequency levels are reached) they will be
at a "deeper level." Once at this level, all sorts of powers
are available to them, from sleep control to psychic healing.
It is vaguely felt that the more complex powers, such as the
psychic healing, are in fact associated with the "deepest"
levels. However, it is worth noting that after the first
meeting where the levels are introduced and such catch phrases
as "Descent into Alpha" (meant to give an adventurous science-
fiction ring to the techniques, which are also talked about as
"soloing through inner space"), the scientific terminology is
dropped altogether and no effort is made to, say, identify

particular levels (e.g. "now you are in theta, now you are in delta").

In analyzing this incorporation of science into doctrine, it is evident that SMC (and other "cult of man" groups) abstract the elements from the scientific context and use them in their own context, which in itself is imaginative and unsystematic.

This represents a technological approach to science, an emphasis on science, not as a perspective, but as a "methodical attainment of a definitely given and practical end by means of an increasingly precise calculation of adequate means" (Gerth and Mills, 1958:293). Such an attitude is also a dimension of rationalization, one that is best illustrated by the role of and effect of industry in this society. In fact, the "cult of man" groups have many similarities to industry. Both are concerned with precision, efficiency and technique. Both are concerned with providing a product while making money. Both are concerned with rationality as pragmatism as opposed to rationality as cognitive system. Both are reacting to a world in which knowledge has become sufficiently fragmented to become neutralized, to become elements isolated from system in the same way (in Durkheimian terms) that social diversification isolates individuals from one another until they appear to have nothing in common. Both business and cult put these pieces back together again in their own arrangement, although the "cult of man" groups reject the development of explanations which would make "sense" out of the new arrangement. In this sense, the rejection of rational systematic thought can hardly be termed irrational. Coupled as it is with the emphasis on technology and pragmatic results, it expresses in fact a predominate attitude of technological society in which industry and bureaucracy defines the framework.

Returning to the question of the relationship between belief and organization in these two groups (the CCR and the "cult of man" groups) it seems clear that the different attitude towards science held by these two groups is related to their economic organization (as it, in turn, reflects secular organization in general). The CCR rejects both on

some levels -- subordinating scientific perspectives and
techniques to religious ones and disassociating themselves
from secular structures and rational economic organization.
On the other hand, the "cult of man" group's use of science,
while ignoring the scientific perspective (science as a world
view) concentrates on scientific techniques, tools and terms
as the most pragmatic and efficient way to attain their own
religious ends. Similarly, as we noted in the last chapter,
they use highly technical/rational methods of financing,
advertising and course organization.

Hence, a comparison of belief and organization in these
two types of groups seems to suggest that the attitude toward
science reflects the degree of rationalism in the economic
structure and meeting format. A review of the attitude toward
science held by the turn-of-the-century cults suggests that as
there are degrees of compromise between religious and economic
structure (noted in the last chapter) so there are also
degrees of accommodation to science.

The turn-of-the-century cults, while accepting science in
general, in fact focused on quite different aspects of science
than do the "cult of man" groups. While they held the credo
that "Science and Religion are a unity" (Mann, 1972:62) they
did not have the same kind of saturation with terminology or
techniques. The occult groups had their own elaborate
terminology, but little of it resembled scientific or social
scientific language. Mann notes the occult groups used such
words as aura, vibration, transmigration, guru and hermetic
and quotes the following passage as exemplary of this esoteric
vocabulary:

> On the word "charge" bring the hands down to your sides
> with dynamic energy but be perfectly relaxed. Visualize
> and feel the GREAT COSMIC STREAMS OF GOLDEN LIGHT
> SUBSTANCE blazing down through you from great BEAMS
> ABOVE you. This is actually taking place, streaming
> like an avalanche through your body, hands and feet,
> flooding into the gas belts below the earth's surface.
> (Mann, 1972:60)

Similarly, the healing techniques of the healing groups
(one of the central techniques of the turn-of-the-century
groups) seemed to be not a backup to, but rather an alternative
to scientific/medical treatment. Finally, none of these groups

used scientific inventions, such as biofeedback machines, to
aid them in their pursuits.

On what then is their claim that "science and religion
are one united" based? The source of this statement seems to
be twofold. On the one hand, it reflects the groups' commitment to being intellectual. Both healing and occult groups
at the turn of the century rejected any sort of emotionalism
(as represented by the sects of that period). Instead, they
represented themselves as rational, calm and committed to the
accumulation and application of a systematic knowledge
(Ellwood, 1973; Mann, 1972; Whitehead, 1975). To this extent
their identification with science was correct. What they
were committed to was science as a perspective, science as a
rational world view. In this sense, they shared with science
a rationality, defined as "the kind of rationalization the
systematic thinker performs on the image of the world: an
increasing theoretical mastery of reality by means of
increasingly precise and abstract concepts" (Gerth and Mills,
1958:293). Accordingly, they rejected disdainfully the shows
of emotion/irrationality of the "born again" Christian.
Finally, they shared with science a practical orientation (as
many magical groups do):

> It was claimed that God's love enabled people to make
> and keep friends. Sermons provided positive
> suggestions on how to become socially acceptable ....
> It is significant that cultists were encouraged to
> seek from God such practical things as prosperity,
> success, poise, happiness and inner peace.
> (Mann, 1972:63)

The turn-of-the-century cults differed from science in
their definition of empirical reality. The occultists and,
to a lesser extent, the healing groups felt that not only the
physical but the metaphysical world was governed by laws that
were discoverable and susceptible to manipulation by man
(sometimes with the help of supernatural figures). They felt
that such understanding (and eventually such power) was to be
gleaned by systematic study:

> Unity and New Thought teachings on the utilization of
> spiritual laws for the attainment of human perfection
> were positively accommodated to the progressive
> outlook of middle class people. This doctrine ascribed
> infinite powers of improvement to spiritually

> enlightened man. Particularly among the occult groups
> the doctrine of perfectibility embraced the goal of
> becoming a genuine metaphysician by the acquisition of
> ever greater esoteric knowledge. (Mann, 1972:65)

Hence, while both science and the turn-of-the-century
groups put man in the same perspective, (the actor in, as
opposed to the reactor to, his environment), the environment
itself was defined differently.

This stance put the turn-of-the-century cults in a
curiously vulnerable position. By accepting the scientific
perspective they were open to being proved wrong by science.
Hence, a good deal of energy was directed to a kind of
competitive attitude toward science. If within the cosmology
of the particular group a systematic explanation could be
found for phenomena which defied scientific explanation, the
cultist felt he had scored a victory. Similarly, if
scientific discoveries or evidence could be used to make a
case for some element of metaphysical reality (say, life after
death) great mileage was exacted by the cult from this data.
However, science could also find a physical explanation for
what the cultist had claimed as a metaphysical reality.
Hence, the attitude toward science was ambivalent. This was
particularly true of the healing groups who were offering an
alternative, not a backup as in the case of the CCR, to
scientific healing. This competitive attitude was underlined
by demanding that members of the Christian Science not
patronize the medical/scientific practitioners and using only
Christian Science practitioners.

It is evident that this ambivalent attitude towards
science and scientists is related to the general attitude to
the secular world. As such it is intimately linked to the
economic and formal organization of these groups.

The turn-of-the-century groups attempted to master the
spiritual world by the accumulation of systematic knowledge,
but very few members even claim to have the experience of
mastery (Ellwood, 1973). Their system, while paying lip-
service to rationality is not efficient or precise in terms
of results. Similarly, while attempting mass marketing in
advertising, the cults' individual chapters or programs were
not standardized enough to package and sell. Too much was
left to the (irrational) discretion of the individual

'lecturer'. Finally, their sources of financing were neither
systematic nor reliable. This approach to the economy may fit
their orientation to the spiritual world, as the scientific
perspective fits their goal of understanding and manipulation.
But neither their organization nor their doctrine were geared
to the level of efficiency, precision, predictability of goal
attainment present in "cult of man" groups.

In sum, we have indicated in this section that in all
three groups the attitude towards science seems directly
expressive of the economic organization of the group (when the
latter is viewed as a measure of rationalisation). CCR
ignores or subordinates both the positivistic orientations of
science and the secular economy. The "cult of man" groups
incorporate the pragmatic or technical aspects of science in
their doctrines and make use of economic rationalism in
equally pragmatic ways. The cults of the turn of the century
fell somewhere in between these two extremes. They adopted
the perspective of science and some of the elements of mass
marketing and course-work format, but they failed to develop
either doctrine or organization to the kind of pragmatic
extremes which might have insured predictable and precise
results.

Healing and Purification

In this section we will turn to the beliefs which may be
seen to flow from the "cult of man" groups' emphasis on
individual as opposed to community development. The specific
doctrine which we will focus on is that of purification and
that of healing. The purification concern may be seen as
reflecting the experience of having the sacred within each
individual. In addition, it reflects the separation of the
individual from the group. Essentially, purification involves
the separation of elements. All "cult of man" groups show
concern about purification.

In contrast, groups such as the CCR which clearly locate
the sacred outside of the self seem to have very little
concern with purification. Rather, most such groups exhibit,
to a greater or lesser extent, a concern with healing. It
will be argued in this section that healing, in contrast with
purification, reflects a desire to join together into larger

wholes. It is a belief which is therefore likely to be found
in a group which emphasizes the importance of community over
individual. It is interesting to note that none of the "cult
of man" groups show similar concerns with healing, with the
exception of the Silva Mind Control group, which we will
discuss in some detail later in this section. Even Psychosynthesis, which ostensibly comes from a therapeutic
tradition, pays little attention to concepts of healing while
centrally concerned with purification.

Healing and Community

For the members of the CCR the ritual of healing, both in
terms of memory healing and physical healing, is very
important to members. The gift of healing is highly valued,
and is granted to some lay members as well as clergy.
Nevertheless, the healing power is seen to flow directly from
God. It is not the responsibility of the healer:

> If we imagine the faucet as the person healing, the
> Spring as God and the water as the gift, then we can
> say that no one ever thanks the faucet for having
> given him water. (Sauve, 1974:80)

Healings do not occur at every meeting, but are usually
requested by a member. If the healing is a mental one, the
healer will put his or her hand on the head of the kneeling
member, while other members of the group gather around laying
their hands also on the head of the ill person or each other,
making a kind of human chain. The healer then recapitulates
the significant events of the patient's life, asking at each
stage that the Lord "heal these wounds." If the healing is
a physical wound, the healer puts his or her hand on or near
the afflicted area.

Most members of the CCR, if they have not had a physical
healing have had a memory healing (which the leader of the
Montreal group indicated was the more "important" of the two).
Members describe the experience as follows:

> In the retreat with Father K. someone asked me if I
> wanted to be prayed over and I said yes. I spoke
> with one of his nuns first about my memories and
> then went to Father K. He said my person had been
> abused at the age of five and that I needed to
> forgive my mother and father. I had never thought of
> this before. I had been too ashamed to tell them.

> In the healing the Father took me in his arms. The
> Father blotted the pain and the negative effect it
> had had in my life. My innocence was restored to me
> and it set me free.
>
> — CCR member

> I had a hard childhood. I had no mother. I cried
> in bed about it and was jealous of others who had a
> mother. I went through the experience of memory
> healing. I walked with God and forgave everyone who
> had hurt me. I remembered even things that I had
> forgotten. It was very beautiful. I felt very good
> after.
>
> — CCR member

> The whole community heals. Ever since the memory
> healing I have felt free. The sense of a block
> removed ...
>
> — CCR member

> I was on retreat. During mass everyone stands around
> the altar. All of a sudden Sister G. said "someone
> is sick." I was having heart trouble ... I couldn't
> speak but I put up my hand. I was sitting and she
> was standing beside me. She put her hand on me ...
> so did others ... in about four minutes praying over
> me the pulse went right back to normal. This is a
> charismatic gift. When you are in the group you can
> feel the pain of someone else.
>
> — CCR member

In all these descriptions there runs the theme of unity.
To be healed is to forgive, to forgive those around you from
whom you have been cut off. In healing you are joined with
lost memories, lost people and literally, the people of the
charismatic community itself. This latter is both physical
and spiritual. The members of a charismatic community can
"feel" each other's pain. They reach out to touch and hold
one another in order to heal that pain. Finally, there is a
sense of a block removed, of being joined to God and to the
sacred.

It is important to note as well, that the healings which
people experience in the community are seen as dependent on
the community. If a member leaves the community, it is
believed he is likely to fall sick again:

> People, of course, talk about what has happened to
> them and tend to bring others with similar problems
> to the prayer meeting. These visitors then ask for
> some sort of prayer for the healing of memories.

They then leave the prayer meeting to return to the
environment where these memories were conceived and
nurtured. As a result, they are not better off than
when they first came to the prayer meeting. (Sauve,
1974:54)

Hence, healing is an experience and a belief which
supports community. It sees sickness in terms of being cut
off from others, either by failing to forgive, by refusing to
open the self to God, by leaving the community. With healing
comes a new wholeness, and that wholeness is represented by a
feeling of being joined to parts of the self and to other
people formerly neglected. In this sense, it may be seen
that the belief in healing flows from and supports the
emphasis on community development rather directly.

For this reason, it is particularly striking that the
"cult of man" groups place little or no emphasis on healing.
While the Charismatics view body and soul as something to be
cured, the "cult of man" groups seem to see both as something
to be protected. In fact, it is difficult to find reference
to illness in "cult of man" literature, with the exception of
Silva Mind Control groups, which we will discuss in detail
later. However, when illness is mentioned, it is seen to
hinge on internal imbalances, or neglect of the self by the
self:

Normally, the imbalance of the instincts creates deep
states of tension and anxiety which are reflected in
our physical body, in our emotional temperament, in
our personal idiosyncracies ... this entire complex
produces in us what we call our personality, an
arbitrary and unpredictable manifestation of the
instinctual imbalance ... personality is our illness,
and we see the world through the anguish of that
sickness.

- Arica pamphlet

Illness comes from disharmony with your own being.
If I feel sick I take it as a sign. Sickness is the
soul guiding itself ... we learn to grow through
what happens to the personality. Sickness could be
prevented if we knew our needs.

- Psychosynthesis member

In order to prevent such disharmony, such imbalance,
"cult of man" groups suggest self-purification:

If we clearly answer our vital and instinctive
questions, our psyche becomes purified and we see
the world exactly as it is. This is the healthy
and essential view, in other words, our natural
and essential state. The Arica system uses
methods for physical cleaning which returns
natural balance to the body ...

- Arica pamphlet

Tonight we are going to talk about mental house-
cleaning. The importance of changing negative to
positive thinking. The biggest step tonight is
to introduce the phrase 'cancel cancel' as a
standard part of the vocabulary. As soon as you
hear something negative you can cancel, cancel.
We don't talk about problems, but about negative
and positive thinking.

- Silva Mind Control lecture

What we're talking about is what it feels like if
you don't deal with your own energy, if you sit
on it. It's like backed up plumbing. Yetch!
Your higher self can't communicate if the plumbing
is backed up ...

- Psychosynthesis member

From these quotes it is obvious that purification is an
internal matter, involving internal reordering, getting in
touch with inner Being, re-establishing balances. There is
no reference made to other people, past or present in this
re-ordering. It is a private matter. In fact, relations
with other people are often seen as activating the personality, causing the imbalance. The symptoms of imbalance are
"habits, hidden fears, physical, emotional and mental
tensions, anxiety, susceptibility, sickness, addiction,
cruelty, erotomania, allergies, phobias and in extreme cases,
psychosis" (Arica pamphlet). In a group such as Psychosynthesis, any emotion displayed in interaction is described
as getting "hooked." The idea of purification is to separate
the emotions and the inner self from the outer personality
which interacts with others, as opposed to identifying with
that personality which can lead to confusion of self with
others, hence the term "hooking."

From this analysis, it would seem that purification
beliefs and attitudes to the body are centrally concerned
with the problem of separation, of cleansing. For adherents
of "cult of man" groups this belief supports the individualist

structure of group life not only because the process is seen as internal and private but because contamination occurs in faulty interaction with other people and things in the outside world. Hence, it discourages the development of community and reinforces the existing individualistic structure.

It is interesting, in this light to examine the one example of a healing ritual present in any of the "cult of man" groups: the psychic healing exercise which ends the Silva Mind Control course. Throughout the course, Silva Mind Control members are told that they can prevent their own ill health by mind control, "positive thought" and repeating such phrases as "I will never learn to contract, either mentally or physically, the disease known as cancer." At the end of the course they are told they can also learn to cure other people by mind control. They simply get a picture of the ill person on their "mental screen" by doing their relaxation techniques. They scan the person mentally to diagnose the illness, then they imagine the illness cured and send the person on their way (mentally).

When comparing this ritual to that of the CCR, two interesting points emerge. The first is that the healing goes on entirely within the person's mind. During the training, the healer works with an "orientologist" who supplies him with the name and age of the person to be healed and who tells him when he has made the correct diagnosis, but no one but the healer sees the sick person, his or her disease or his or her cure. Related to this, and more important, the SMC students are told specifically that "we do not perform psychic investigation of a person when that person is present" and "we do not give our own name to be worked as a case while we are present." For the students in the class, this means that the cases that they do are people they have never heard of and never seen. This, according to the SMC beliefs, is one of the proofs that psychic healing goes on: the person healing is able to visualize, diagnose and cure a person he has never seen, and most likely never will. The connections between people, particularly between members of the group is practically non-existent, as is any confrontation with the physical reality of disease. The sick

people appear as parts of the internal world of the healer
which he "bathes in white light" and sends away. Little
effort is made by members even to check if a cure "in the
world" was in fact effected. Hence, it could be argued that
for all intents and purposes this "healing" ritual is in fact
another type of purification in which elements present within
the individual are cleansed and separated out, with little
reference to the real relationships between people evident in
the charismatic healing ritual, or indeed in most accepted
healing rituals, medical or religious.

In sum, then, when comparing the CCR groups with the
"cult of man" movements, we find very different approaches to
the physical and mental "health." The former is curative,
the latter preventative. The former sees the problems as
stemming from the individual cutting himself off from others,
failing to forgive, failing to open himself to God. The
latter sees the problem in terms of internal imbalances and
contaminations, stemming from the confusion of inner and outer
self, of self and others. The answer is reuniting with the
community in the former case; in the latter, it is avoiding
getting hooked by others in the community and looking inward
to re-establish balance.

If we consider the turn-of-the-century groups in the
light of this opposition, there appears to be a split between
groups. Mann has noted that there were two kinds of groups:
the healing groups and the occult groups. Of the two, the
healing groups became the more established in the course of
time. Groups such as Christian Science which endured, became
more sect-like in terms of their demands for total commitment
of their members. Their healing ritual is interesting in the
light of the contrast between the SMC and the CCR rituals.
While there was no physical contact between patient and
healer, nonetheless, they were usually in the same room. In
a private interaction involving only patient and healer (not
the community at large) the healer tuned into the mind of the
patient, becoming one with him and so healing him. This
ritual provides a fascinating combination of the two extremes
we discussed earlier. Like SMC, the healing was mental,
involving the ability of the healer somehow to join himself
mentally with his patient. Like SMC, all illness was seen as

due to negative thought or idea habits. Unlike SMC, but like
the CCR, this negative thinking was seen as involving a
cutting off of the self from God. Like CCR, the correction
of this condition involved the patient voluntarily opening
himself to another member of the community. The ritual hence
fell midway between the two oppositions of purification and
healing. It also reflected the group organization of the
turn-of-the-century healing cults: the relationship between
members was not as strong as the sects past and present but
between leader and follower, the links were much stronger
than in the "cult of man" groups.

On the other hand, the occult groups made little or no
reference to healing. Most of these groups, however, had
elements of gnosticism (like many of the "cult of man" groups)
and so were centrally concerned with the contamination which
could result from interaction with the people and things of
the external world:

> ... the objective and purpose of the efforts of the
> Gnostic is to establish an effective conscious
> contact with this ultimate Source of Power and Life,
> which resides constantly at the very back of our
> consciousness and therefore is always available.
> This unobstructed contact can only be established
> when the dominion of the rulers is broken, that is,
> when man is no longer subject to the attachments and
> fascinations of the lower world of sense perceptions,
> emotions and analytical reason, but having trans-
> cended the latter, has put on the 'vesture of light'
> and thus has accomplished what modern analytical
> psychology calls total integration. (Ellwood, 1973:118)

What is interesting is that organizationally the occult
groups were more loosely organized than the healing groups,
putting less emphasis on community than the latter. This
fact seems to support our general theory, as does the fact,
pointed out by Mann, that the drift of membership over time
was away from the healing groups and towards the occult
groups (seldom did members of the occult groups go to the
healing groups). It may be suggested that the looser, more
individualistic structure and doctrine of the occult groups
became more reflective of the organization of the larger
society as the differentiation and specialization, which
marks our society, continued to advance.

In closing this discussion of the healing and purification beliefs and their relation to social structure, it is interesting to note, in passing, the case of Scientology. Scientology presents a particularly instructive case because it is a group which has existed for a comparatively long time and only in its later phases of development has come to clearly identify the sacred as within the individual. It provides an example of a single group in which the belief system has evolved to fit changes in the organizational structure in the predicted manner. A brief review of this process may hence provide longitudinal data that supplements the cross-sectional data we have reviewed.

Scientology has one of the longer histories of any of the current cults. It was established in or around 1949, under the name Dianetics. Between then and the mid-nineteen fifties, it proliferated as a number of loosely connected groups centered around auditors who were trained by the Foundation and its founder-leader, L. Ron Hubbard. The fees were minimal and along with the actual organization of the individual group, left largely to the discretion of the individual leader. The doctrine was a systematic view of the human mind which drew a great deal from Freudian analysis (Wallis, 1977). The aim of the group was to treat individuals therapeutically to rid them of 'engrams' acquired through traumas in their youth and to which they were still reacting, which were programming their current responses. The treatment was a lengthy therapeutic process with an auditor to search back through the patients' past and root out these engrams through a series of systematically developed diagnostic and analytic techniques. The result was a 'clear' patient, one who used the 'analytic' as opposed to the 'reactive' mind to make decisions. The clear patient was also free of physical and mental illness.

> The purpose of Dianetic therapy, therefore, was to gain access to and locate engrams, and 'erase' them from the reactive mind, thus eradicating their effects in the form of psychosomatic illness, emotional tension or lowered capability. (Wallis, 1977:23)

Adherents who had experienced this treatment, spoke of improved health and well-being. The theory also included a series of levels or dynamics, the highest of which was "the urge toward survival as a part of or ward of a Supreme Being" (Wallis, 1977:39).

In the early fifties, due to organizational difficulties, Dianetics underwent the change to become Scientology. This change involved both the organization and the beliefs of the movement. Organizationally, Scientology represented the bureaucratization of the movement. "Boards of Directors, ill-regulated and salaried staffs, and irreverent wives were things of the past" (Whitehead, 1975:580). Scientology became centralized and standardized. The loose structure was replaced by a well-defined coursework format, with set fees for each course. The groups were turned into classes from which one graduated. What was taught in the courses was pre-programmed, and auditors could not practice independently (Wallis, 1977; Malko, 1971; Whitehead, 1975).

The changes which the beliefs underwent were of con-siderable interest to the subject of this thesis. In the first place, the systematic and positivist orientation of Dianetics was abandoned:

> Accordingly, he (L. Ron Hubbard) openly reversed his position on the material nature of the psyche and began to develop a set of ideas that would account not only for past lives and the wild assortment of incidents which people found in their earlier life-times, but also for the whole range of uncanny phenomena which have hitherto been relegated to the realm of the supernatural. (Whitehead, 1975:580-81)

In accordance with this acceptance of uncanny phenomena, Scientology departed from Dianetics in that it posited that humans had within themselves the potential to become 'Operating Thetans' -- i.e. divine. With this notion the conception of 'clear' shifted slightly. It was no longer a state of having been healed of past engrams; instead it became the state of developing more of this inner potential. Accordingly, auditing became less important and less lengthy. While the emphasis on positivism diminished, Scientology became more preoccupied with technology. The E-Meter, a sensory device, was introduced into the auditing process to speed up the detection of problem areas in the personality. As well, an increased emphasis was placed on the technology of communication, on being able to type or class other people

and on being able to communicate like a machine with utmost
technical proficiency. Inherent in this seemed to be a desire
to avoid contamination in interpersonal relations. One
graduate of the communications course expressed this as
follows:

> I am no longer afraid of causing an unwanted effect
> on another being. This Grade has cleared out such
> a lot of garbage I knew was there, but I never could
> put my finger on, and so was therefore the effect of
> it. I feel great knowing that it is gone. (Wallis,
> 1977:120)

This brief summary of the development of Scientology is
meant to indicate that as the structure of a single group
changed from irrational to rational, its use of science
changed from empirical system to technological device. Its
image of the sacred moved from without to within and its
emphasis moved from a kind of patient-client healing therapy
reminiscent of Christian Science, to an emphasis on purity of
relations, of inner state and of individual power.

The Integrated Self vs. the "Cast of Thousands"

Closely related to the previous belief dimension is a
feature conspicuous because of its presence in the "cult of
man" groups and its absence elsewhere. This is the belief in
internal fragmentation or the "cast of thousands" -- a belief
quite opposite from that held by the CCR and reflecting, it
may be argued, both the partiality and the transience of the
"cult of man" organization.

One of the elements of most pentacostal and sect-like
groups, which the CCR imitates, is the experience of being
'born again' as a whole new person. The experience, as
described by the initiates, is one of self-discovery, of
feeling whole, 'filled' with the Spirit, doubts and confusion
washed away (Gerlach and Hines, 1970). Members of the
Montreal CCR groups described their reactions to the Baptism
of the Spirit which marked their official entry into the
group as follows:

> It was like a rebirth. There was tremendous love.
> I was a new person. It changed things -- it really
> happened. It was as if I met God.
>
> $\qquad\qquad\qquad\qquad$ - CCR member

Something wonderful happened. I was emptied of sin --
I had an awareness of who I was. It was like a beam
of light. The first thing was the depth of awareness
of my own self -- it caused a lot of pain. Joy came
slowly as I was emptied of sin. The joy was the
realization of the darkness that the Lord had brought
me out of.

- CCR member

It was at a retreat. The experience was a dissolving
... the hardnesses were softened. I cried a lot --
it was like a washing. I felt heat. I felt love
from all the people who were praying over me and I
felt love for them.

- CCR member

There is a sense of homecoming, rebirth, awakening in all
these descriptions that seems to describe a person 'coming to
himself' in the presence of God. It was identity forming: a
new person in a new relationship, but a wholer, more
integrated person than before. The 'I was lost but now I'm
found' theme is so common to this type of group that it has
become another cliché.

In contrast, the training received in the "cult of man"
groups hinges on an interesting phenomenon: the recognition
by members that within them dwells not one but a multitude of
different people and/or personalities.

Psychosynthesis, for instance, talks about the number of
sub-personalities. In addition to the Higher Self and the
personality which acts in the world, there is a great
splintering of self of which the student gradually becomes
aware. These sub-personalities are seen as being at war with
each other, in need of another presence which is judge and
mediator:

All of us have a large number of what might be called
sub-personalities. These are aspects of ourselves
which emerge in different situations, called forth by
the varying roles we play in life and these are often
quite inconsistent with one another. When we say "I"
it is rarely the voice of the true Self speaking but
rather one of the sub-personalities. These partial
aspects of ourselves have a way of making decisions
and promises which commit the whole person, and we
may find ourselves in conflict when one of the sub-
personalities refuses to honor a commitment made by
a contradictory one, leaving us in a state of inner
civil war.

- Psychosynthesis handbook

It is interesting to note that these sub-personalities are permanent fixtures of the interior landscape. The goal of Psychosynthesis is not to eliminate them but to balance them.

Groups like est and Silva Mind Control have other sorts of internal landscapes. In the case of SMC, these are a male and a female which materialize in the internal imaginary 'lab' which the student has created. These guides will thereafter be available at all times for consultation on psychic matters. In addition, due to the abilities of the SMC member to bring any other existing person into her 'lab' and so project them on the 'mental' screen, there is a sense which members have of being continually in tune with internal millions:

> ... There are an awful lot of sick people floating around out there in need of help and the psychic might get the wrong person altogether on the screen. Fine tuning only comes with practice. If you get the wrong person don't worry ... just heal that person and send him on his way ...
>
> - Silva Mind Control - instructor

This sense of a floating sea of people directly connected to the internal world of the student is very prominent in the literature of Shakti and Arica. Both these groups are very concerned with past lives of members. One of the aims of Shakti is to eliminate the blocks in Consciousness so that the individual can become aware of all the past selves that have inhabited his or her body, as well as all the bodies the present 'soul' has inhabited which is termed "total recall of the entire Being-history." Arica, too, seeks moments at 'Higher Levels' when they are mentally united with others' present and past selves, as well as their own. At level +6 (a very high level) Arica members are not only linked to their two spirit guides (Lilly, 1972:214) but to other people past and present:

> At a certain point of the trip in Chile, I was doing an ego reduction with another man. He had found a bit of my ego and I went up quite automatically into Satori +6 while holding in +4 and +12. The part of me in +6 took a look around and saw that part of him was peaking into +6 but that he didn't know it. I came back down and reported this to him, including one sentence on having met him before in a previous

> life. He apparently wasn't aware of the part of him-
> self that went into +6. He became extremely angry
> upon hearing me talk about previous lives in which
> his self-metaprogrammer does not believe; he broke
> off our contact. (Lilly, 1972:216)

> I realized that all Essences are connected to one
> another on level 6 and are in communication whether
> one's self knows this or not. They also share past
> histories of each self. (Ibid.:214)

For Arica members as well, reaching the higher levels of consciousness means becoming aware of an internal "cast of thousands."

This sense of internal diversity is one of the most interesting aspects of the beliefs of the "cult of man" movements. Ellwood (1973) has pointed out that occult groups often present members with spirit helpers. However, in general, these helpers locate themselves outside the individual. For example, the Theosophists posited the existence of a group of Masters, "those great mediating figures who represent individuals much more highly evolved than the ordinary person." Much of the Theosophist training is to develop psychic and occult powers which will help them contact these masters and use their powers. However, the Masters remain outside entities that the Theosophist may visit in spirit. Similarly, the Spiritualists have a series of Levels in their cosmology. At each level dwell different spirits, astral entities, angels, angel loved ones, invisible friends, messengers, spirit helpers, guides (in descending order). Not all spiritualists can tune into these levels; for most, they can only contact these higher beings through the medium. The medium himself may contact these entities only if they so will. The spirits have an existence and a will outside the medium (even though they make their appearance through the mind of the medium) (Zaretsky, I, 1975:209). Hence, unlike Arica, this cast of thousands (a) is not available to everyone; (b) is not an inherent part of the internal landscape of the individual, available to be tuned into any time the individual chooses. For the turn-of-the-century cults, the individual, herself, was not seen as a collection of spirits or personalities.

Once again this belief seems to share elements of both the contemporary "cult of man" groups and the sect. The spiritual world was seen as heavily populated and it was deemed possible for the human individual to tune in to this plurality. The plurality, however, did not exist within the individual; like the CCR members, the individual was visited by the supernatural. The turn-of-the-century cults retained at least some autonomy of action in the spirits and some of the sense of the integration of self that marks the charismatic experience.

While the relationship is not as direct as in the previous two cases, it may be argued that this contrast between internal integration and internal diversity on the belief level corresponds to the organizational dimension of total versus partial identification. The way in which the sect demands total identification, to the extent that even friendships with people outside the cult tend to wither away, also produces a very strong and unified reference group for identity formation. On the other hand, the kind of compromises which the "cult of man" makes with the secular world and secular values, the way in which the individual takes her knowledge gained in the cult back out into the world instead of bringing the world for reinterpretation by the cult, means that the "cult of man" member still faces the problem of establishing identity in terms of a number of competing reference systems. Note in the above quote about Psychosynthesis that the sub-personalities are seen as 'called forth by the varying roles we play in life'. The belief in the cast of thousands may well flow from the experience of partial identification which the organization of the movement (and of the technological society which it mirrors) encourages. Similarly, the belief in the ability of the leader in the turn-of-the-century occult groups to at least contact the myriad of spiritual beings in the universe, flowed from the organization which stressed the leader-disciple relation. The beliefs of the turn-of-the-century groups suggested that the boundaries are fluid, but they haven't disappeared. Similarly, their organization, while fluid, demanded more commitment than the "cult of man" groups do. If nothing else, the membership did not seem to have as many competing allegiances as the "cult of man" members. This issue will be dealt with in greater detail in the next chapter.

The above beliefs may also be seen to flow from the permanent-transient opposition which we discussed in organizational terms. This opposition can be seen as inextricably linked to both the community vs. individual development and the total vs. partial identification aspects of group organization. In other words, the transient nature of group life, formally limited by the coursework structure, seems by definition to result in an emphasis on individual development and on partial identification. Similarly, the cast of thousands' belief is not only a way of expressing an identity based on pluralistic social organization but also an identity based on a continuously shifting social organization.

More specifically, the transience-permanence opposition seems linked to a certain aspect of the cast of thousands' belief: the degree to which the past and/or future person-alities of the individual member are seen to be present in the internal landscape of that individual as active figures to which she ought to be able to relate. This, of course, implies at least some support for the notion of reincarnation. A firm belief in the resurrection of the soul as found in the CCR mitigates against the notion of the multiplicity of selves. However, the interest in reincarnation is given a special twist in the instance of the "cult of man" groups which believe in it. Many of the turn-of-the-century cults, while believing in reincarnation, did not attempt to recapture an awareness of these selves simultaneous with this present existence. The eastern groups which support the notion of reincarnation, see it often as a condition to escape, not to reclaim and experience. But the "cult of man" groups, which search out their own past and future personalities in their present selves, see such simultaneous awareness as control, overcoming the forgetfulness of death. And the notion is most highly developed in the "cult of man" group which places greatest emphasis on organizational transience: Shakti.

As we noted in the previous chapter, Shakti often dissolves groups in mid-course and then sets up shop under a new name. E. Gold, the leader of the group, is also intensely preoccupied with the past and future lives of members, of the problem of death and rebirth under a different form. In his latest book, the American Book of the Dead, Gold describes in detail the problems of the transition from death to rebirth, in order that these can be subject to the control of the individual. This interest can be seen as an extension of the Shakti desire to 'unfold the soul' so that the individual can become conscious during Between World Flights, able to choose the next body and eliminate "massive memory blackouts" which cause the individual to forget his previous life or lives (Palmer, 1975:64). The exercises developed in Shakti are all orientated (like Gold's book) to "the formation of a Being able to 'consciously Determine and Direct the Genetic Code Module Package'," able in other words, to remember his past lives and the transition from one to another. This developed belief system quite clearly is related to the continual process of death and rebirth of the group organization itself, in other words, the transience of the group. The 'cast of thousands' as a collection of past and future identities, seems also to reflect transience vs. permanence. Shakti's latest offering is a correspondence course in the art of dying.

In conclusion, we have tried in this chapter to describe some features of the belief systems of the "cults of man" which separate these groups both from other new religious movements of the sect variety and turn-of-the-century cults. In addition, we have attempted to demonstrate that these beliefs are directly related to the organizational elements of group life which distinguished these groups from others. These relationships are summarized in Table 2.

We have tried to show that the emphasis on scientific technology reflects a rationalized economic organization, that the emphasis on purification reflects the individual-istic style of the organization and that the belief in internal fragmentation reflects the pluralistic organization of these cults. Finally, we have noted that while no specific belief alone seems to represent the transient nature of group life, elements of this transience appear to be reflected in the clear emphasis on the idea of the internal "cast of thousands" (particularly when members of this cast, as they often are, are representatives of past lives).

By comparison we have suggested that the above beliefs
are clearly opposed to those held by the CCR who also occupy
the opposing position on the organizational continuum.
Finally, we have suggested that the cults of the turn-of-the-
century which fall somewhere in the middle on the organizational continuum, also held beliefs which were a mixture of
these opposing views and which in turn seem nicely to reflect
their own unique organization.

In the next chapter we will leave the comparative
framework we have used in the past two chapters and take a
closer look at the "cult of man" groups alone, at the way
their organization and beliefs reflect not only each other,
but the larger social structure of which they are a part.
We will also examine the way in which the beliefs described
in this chapter are all aspects of that central belief,
which Durkheim suggested was expressive of the diversification and specialization of the modern world: the location
of the sacred within the human individual.

Table 2

Hypothesized Relationship between the Character of Social
Organization and Corresponding Beliefs in "Cult of Man,"
Turn-of-the-Century and Charismatic Renewal Groups

	Character of Social Organization	Corresponding Belief
"Cult of Man"	rationalized economic structure: fee for coursework	emphasis on science as technology
	emphasis on individual development	corner with contamination and purity
	partial involvement of members	internal cast of thousands past personalities important
	transient community life	
turn-of-the century cults	structure semi-rationalized advertising pseudo lecture format failure to use methods to secure continuity of group	acceptance of science as an orientation, failure to 'use' technology to achieve ends
	leader-disciple relationship	concern with healing on a one-to-one basis; healer-client
	membership with few competing involvements although total commitment not demanded	internal sense of unity except for 'mediums' - leaders able to contact casts of spiritual helpers
	groups short-lived but not deliberately terminated	-individual's own past personalities exist but don't figure in cast
Catholic Charismatic Renewal	structure irrational	science subordinated to religious means and ends
	group links very important	concern with healing of each other, all members participate in ritual
	total commitment demanded	internal unity individual not seen as having had previous lives or personalities but in attempting to attain "eternal life."
	group life seen as infinite	

CHAPTER VII

BEHIND THE FACES: POLLUTION FEARS AND THE NOTION OF THE SACRED IN "CULT OF MAN" GROUPS

In this chapter we will return to a consideration of the central and identifying feature of the "cult of man" groups: their definition of the sacred as lying within the individual. We will begin with a more detailed description of the notion of the sacred which the groups hold. We will then attempt an interpretation of the appeal of these beliefs and by implication, the relationship of the belief system of the "cult of man" groups and the larger North American social structure from which members are drawn and which shape the experience of these members.

One feature of religious experience which Durkheim fails to develop in his discussion of the "cult of man," but which he discusses at some length in Elementary Forms is the sacred/profane dichotomy. In primitive religion, Durkheim saw this opposition as central:

> ... two classes which embrace all that exists but which radically exclude each other. Sacred things are those which the interdictions protect and isolate; profane things, those to which the interdictions are applied and which must remain at a distance from the first. Religious beliefs are the representations which express the nature of sacred things and the relations which they sustain, either with each other or with profane things. Finally, rites are the rules of conduct which prescribe how men should behave in relation to sacred things. (Durkheim, 1961:56)

In discussing the "cult of man," Durkheim makes reference to this sacred/profane split, only indirectly, by suggesting that the human individual (idealized) will be "invested with that mysterious property which creates an empty space around holy objects which keeps them from profane contacts and draws them from ordinary life" (Durkheim, 1969:21). Elsewhere, he makes it clear that it is not the 'individual personality' which will be worshipped or held sacred, however. Rather, it is the qualities of idealized humanity in each person. Where these qualities will be located so that a space is drawn around them which separates them from the profane contacts (which one must assume includes the individual personality) Durkheim does not make clear.

In the previous chapter in which we examined some of the central beliefs of the "cult of man" groups, however, the location and relationship of sacred to profane has become somewhat clearer. It is as if the line dividing the two lies within the individual human being. Indeed, it is her 'outer' personality which is associated with the profane and her inner 'Being' wherein she is joined to all humanity in her perfection and limitless potential which contains the sacred.

The most immediate and obvious effect of having sacred and profane coexistent in the same body is an intense concern with the problem of contamination. Durkheim suggested that the relationship of sacred and profane are governed in both positive and negative ways. Positive rituals allowed for intercourse between sacred and profane; negative prevented contamination.

When sacred and profane are so spatially intimate, the emphasis is inevitably negative; the prevention of contamination becomes all-important. This has been true in the past of gnostic movements (to which the "cult of man" groups have been compared) (Ellwood, 1973). Past gnostic movements, however, which shared this trait of seeing Man as both sacred and profane, believed Man was a spark of light or divinity encapsulated in a profane envelope of flesh which tied him to this world. The sacred element of Man was associated with his powers for rational and intellectual thought, whereas the profane was his instinctual nature, including his physical body (Ellwood, 1973; Brown, 1975). Great pains were then taken to subdue the body and develop the intellect in order that the former would not contaminate the latter.

In contrast, the "cult of man" groups have almost reversed the labelling of most gnostic groups. For them, the profane is the rational mind and the sacred is the deeper instinctual nature and the body. One obvious explanation for this reversal is the fact that the outer material world, which is also held to be profane, has become increasingly less natural, more artificial, technological, man-made and 'disenchanted'. It could be argued that for gnostic-type

movements (those which locate both sacred and profane within
the individual) the aspect of the human make-up which is most
similar to the outer world and the order of that world is
seen as profane, while that which seems 'not of this world' is
seen as the location of the sacred. Hence for the "cult of
man" drawing its support from the dwellers of large cosmopolitan cities in which most, if not all 'natural' processes
and things have been replaced by man-made artifacts and
technology, the rational conscious mind which built this
world and the 'personality' that operates in it are seen as
profane whereas the deeper instincts and flesh and blood body
become the sacred.

> For archaic man, and for most religion through the
> ages, nature has been real, but not in itself sacred.
> It has been rather the "enemy," identified with pri-
> mordial chaos, which man subdues to create the sacred
> as ordered human society -- the city with the temple in
> its midst.
> Now, however, in a return to a new form of cosmic
> religion nature has become the sacred and the city the
> profane. It was not actually likely that the "secular
> city" would become the sacred, for the sacred is always
> that which is hidden, inaccessible, rare ... (Ellwood,
> 1973:303)

Unlike the gnostic groups, therefore, the "cult of man"
movements are not physical ascetics. They are not trying to
subdue the body or the instincts to protect the rational mind.
Instead, as we will see in subsequent chapters on ritual,
they aim to subdue the latter to protect the former. They
aim to keep body and being 'pure' from the contamination of
the machine world and all its 'wastes'.

The notion of purity, which we described in the last
chapter, articulates in the most direct manner the problem of
possible contamination which the proximity of sacred and
profane in the individual creates. As we noted, this last
notion involves both a private dimension of self-purification
(one maintains a space around the sacred by a careful
balancing and neutralizing of profane elements which otherwise
run riot and take over the individual) and an interactional
dimension (in which one carefully detaches the Inner Self from
participation in contaminating interactions with others). It
is both these dimensions which have undoubtedly been the
source of the theories labelling the "cult of man" groups as

more narcissistic and individualistic than other new religious
movements.

However, if Durkheim is correct, the location of the
sacred within the individual is not only a result of "having
nothing in common" (i.e. an expression of societal specialization and diversity) but also an expression of what people
still have in common: their essential humanity. The attitude
toward the sacred found in these groups should therefore tell
us something not only about the members as individuals but
about members as part of a larger social group.

We will now turn to a more precise examination of the
attitude toward the sacred, which is characterized in these
groups by a central preoccupation with the prevention of
pollution and/or contamination. While this seems on the
surface to suggest a fear of interpersonal contacts as one
source of contamination, on the other hand, there is evidence
in the advertising literature and in the statements of members
themselves of an intense longing for interpersonal contacts.
It seems that the members suffer from contradictory impulses:
to seek out and to avoid intimate contact. In this sense
'ideal of community' which some theorists have identified and
the 'privatism' mentioned by others are both experienced by
the members themselves.

In order to understand how these seemingly contrary
positions relate in the group belief system, and what they
reflect about social relations we will, in the remainder of
this chapter, take a closer look at pollution fears in "cult
of man" groups and what they communicate about the members'
experience in society at large.

The Hunger for Close Encounters

Researchers who have studied the "cult of man" groups,
leaders of the groups and members themselves, all admit that
one of the main drives for joining the movements is to meet
new people or to improve the existing relations. A survey of
est participants indicated that 79.9% of participants joined
with the expectation that they would be able to have "better
relationships with family and friends" (Ornstein, 1975) and
Wallis (1977) notes that for recruits to Scientology, "problems
of interpersonal relations were prominent sources of motivation

to seek help" (Wallis, 1977:170). The groups themselves are
obviously aware of this appeal and play up to it in their
advertising. Scientology terms itself:

> The keys to understanding the human mind and human
> nature. With them you have the Vital Knowledge
> necessary to understanding others, handling them
> and establishing sane, growing relationships.
> (Wallis, 1977:162)

Silva Mind Control suggests it will improve your business
and personal relationships. Arica offers a special course on
Understanding the Couple, claiming that "Beyond the failure
of the conventional couple, a whole new style of relationship
opens up based on honesty, respect and love: the evolutionary
couple" (Arica pamphlet).

The leaders of the groups often freely admit that
initially the group provides a kind of Lonely Hearts Club:
"People come here looking for companionship. They tend to
latch onto that as a first way of setting up an environment"
(Palmer, 1976:37). Est is acknowledged to be a good place to
meet eligible people of the opposite sex (Greene, 1976; Bry,
1976). The members themselves describe their attraction to
the group in terms of a longing to somehow get closer to
people.

> I joined Psychosynthesis because I didn't feel like I
> was giving or getting love ... my needs weren't being
> met and I know I wasn't meeting other people's needs,
> which was sad because I wanted to. I wanted to find
> out what was blocking me.
>
> — Psychosynthesis member

> I took the est training because I am really nervous
> about my job and I wanted to get over that. Some of
> my friends had taken it and they appeared to have
> gotten a lot out of it. Besides, they would all sit
> around and talk and laugh about their experiences in
> a language that seemed to leave me out a little. I
> figured I would go out and get the training and then
> I could really be with them and experience what they
> were experiencing.
>
> — est member

> I leafed through the book (on Arica) and saw that it
> was underlined and thought that maybe I could get to
> know more about the girl by reading it. So I
> borrowed it.
>
> — Arica member

The sense of being blocked, excluded from normal interchange with other people characterizes many of the testimonies
of members. There seems to be a "barrier to trust," something
keeping the member from the kind of contact he would like to
have. He is in search of some "key of understanding," which,
as in the last quote, will somehow open himself or other
people so that an interchange and/or relationship might
develop.

According to the beliefs of the "cult of man" groups,
the block which keeps people from "experiencing life" being
"in tune with the world" or "meeting other people," is that
'profane' part of ourselves, the 'personality' or 'ego', the
outer aspect with which we habitually interrelate. Silva Mind
Control terms it the 'beta mind'; est, Arica call it the
'ego', Psychosynthesis and Shakti call it the 'personality',
but leaders, literature and members all identify it as the
source of the difficulty in getting 'close' to other people
and to life in general.

The problem with the 'ego', as seen by these groups, is
that it is a machine or robot, reacting and acting purely
mechanically to people and situations. It is built out of
societal norms, old traumas, old behavior patterns.

> Unfortunately, most people never have a chance to
> develop their instincts. The society which teaches
> us skills we need in order to survive also con-
> ditions us to behavior patterns which cover our
> instincts so that instead of feeling in tune with
> the world we feel afraid in it, imitating others
> and deceiving ourselves.
>
> - Arica pamphlet

It continues through the routines and daily games, "our acts"
which keep our instinctual or essential selves from developing
and growing with which we deceive ourselves and others. The
'ego' is hence seen as a tyrant which runs a house it doesn't
own.

> Gold (E. J. Gold, the group founder of Shakti) sees the
> divine essence as a seed that must be worked on in order
> to grow. The reason so few people grow a soul is that
> they are so caught up in their routines and daily games.
> There are blockages, nerve disorders in the body which
> stop growth. So what Shakti was trying to do was to
> shock people out of their routines, their conditioned
> beliefs, patterns, responses, so they could have a good

look at themselves, at what they were doing ... Ego is
repressed in order to give Being a chance to grow ....

- Shakti member

After the training, I began to realize what an "act" I
was running. I claimed to be such a private person
because I was really afraid to admit that I needed
other people. At the time it was more important for
me to be cool and sophisticated, without ever letting
anyone get too close. Now, I understand that this
'privacy number' is an excuse to prevent myself from
being in touch with what is going on. It's a barrier
to experiencing life.

- est member

Finally, the problem is created by the ego-quality of
rational and analytic thought, which sees life as a history,
a series of events, which attempts always to interpret or
explain.

Its usually the ego that does the talking about personal history. If put aside, it won't get in the way
and more attention is focused on what else is going
on.

- Shakti member

-- an ego is a point of view attempting to cause its
own survival. So its purpose is to dominate everything and everybody ... thinking you know is an actual
barrier to experience.

- Werner Erhard, est founder

... rational thought paralyzes everything. Reality
doesn't happen that way. In reality everything flows.
This means that your reason is not matching reality.
When that happens you enter the endless process of the
chattering of the mind that in Arica we know as
dokosis or the strength of the imagination so out of
control that it forms opinions about anything and
everything.

- Oscar Ichazo, Arica

Hence, the personality or ego is seen as an accumulation
of roles or 'acts' or sub-personalities, made up in turn of
preconceptions, old anxieties, patterns, responses, behavior
patterns with which we attempt to deal with the world and
relate to others. We pin our conception of reality onto
reality and therefore fail to see what is real or essential,
either in ourselves or in others. The result, according to
"cult of man" groups, is that we are isolated, lonely,
hungering after contact which we prevent ourselves from having.

From this image of the personality and interpersonal relations, it is easy to understand why some theorists would believe these groups to be counterculture and compensatory. What seems to be described is alienated individuals hungering for close community and joining a movement which addresses itself to the problem and provides such a community. People who resent the impersonality and technological emphases of modern life, drop the roles for more 'real', impulsive relationships. However, the description does not end here. In equal proportion to the amount of hunger for personal contacts, there is found in members and in the literature of groups, a fear of such contacts bordering on the pathological.

The Fear of Close Encounters

Members talk incessantly of being unable to trust others, of longing to be closer but fearing to do so, of needing "less protection":

> I feel I've got to be careful ... don't feel ... less protection, I'd like to have less protection .... I'd like to sit close but I don't have the guts .... I'd like to sit closer .... The last two or three times (meetings) the group was dead ... everyone was careful what to say ... I'm careful what I say. I've chickened out. There's been times I wanted to say things, wonder if it would be helpful and don't say it ... now that I'm talking about it I feel sadness.
>
> - Psychosynthesis member

In the above quote, it is interesting to note, a double fear is felt: there is a fear both for the self, "I need less protection," and a fear for others: "I'm careful what I say ... wonder if it would be helpful." What is feared is not precisely named although it seems to have something to do with "feeling" and with "saying" and with physical proximity (although this may be purely metaphoric in the above quote). The fear may be better understood by looking closer at its two aspects: the danger to self and the danger to others.

The danger to self seems to come from being 'drained' and from being 'controlled'. Both seem to be aspects of involvement with others. One member of Arica noted that he felt relieved when he met other Aricans for the first time:

> I really liked the Arica people. With the people at the Coop (where the member had worked) there was a

lot of random energy ... I felt like I was being
sucked dry ... trying to organize things. With the
Aricans the energy didn't dissipate.

- Arica member

Another fear was that of letting another individual get
too close, for fear they would take you over. For example,
in one of the healing exercises in a Silva Mind Control group,
the healing psychic, Maria, doing her first case, got the
picture of a sick woman "on her mental screen." She was
supposed merely to diagnose the woman's health problem and
"send her on her way." Instead, she became very upset because
the woman in her mind would not "tell me what was wrong." She
began to cry uncontrollably. Her 'orientologist', who also
happened to be the group instructor, became very agitated. He
kept telling her "Turn down the emotional volume! Remember
it's your mind, Maria. You are in control." Maria persisted
in weeping. She didn't feel in control at all.

While in this case it was an imagined woman (at least
one no one but Maria could see) that got control of her mind,
this danger is felt by groups to be present in interaction
with others even when these 'others' are physically embodied.

What we choose to think about energizes those thoughts.
If I'm not making that choice, other people can manipulate me ... they make it for me ... you can use some
levels of energy to manipulate others, to take away
their free will. That happens all the time with mental
energies ...

- Psychosynthesis member

In addition to others being able to manipulate and drain
the self, the self is seen as able to exude a kind of poison
which can contaminate others. This is expressed most vividly
in reference to that most intimate relationship of the mother
and unborn child:

We are charging that kid that is inside the mother all
the time with the negativity that is around. From the
very beginning. Because there is nothing that really
absorbs more than the fetus ... it's absorbing all the
time ... all ... absolutely all ... the lacks that the
parents have. Suppose a baby can be charged negatively
inside the womb, because of the blood of the mother.
If the mother is in the passions ... the blood of the
baby is going to be charged by passion. It comes to
the world already suffering ... because the child is
like a sponge ...

- Arica leader

This ability to contaminate others goes beyond the mother-baby relationship, however. It comes from being "off centre" from looking to the outside for what can only be found inside, from being 'in ego' as opposed to being 'in essence'. In 'ego' the individual exudes dangers:

> Generally such people (people out of touch with their Higher Selves) see the power as outside themselves and with others. They feel their needs are not being met because of others. And, of course, their needs aren't being met because in such a state you <u>repel exactly what you want. You put out such negativity that you repel what you want.</u> (Emphasis mine)
>
> - Psychosynthesis leader

In summary, the adherents of these movements can see themselves as dangerous and endangered. The danger seems to be in the form of 'energy' but it is energy when mixed with 'attachment' -- passions or feelings and linked to the personality. Only by detachment and 'disidentification' can an individual avoid this danger to himself and to others.

> We are dominated by everything with which our self is identified. We can dominate and control everything from which we disidentify ourselves ...
>
> - Shakti member

> These are the ground rules: Share from our own experi- ence, don't generalize, use the word 'I'. Don't dump on another person, don't unload all your stuff on them. This is called owning our own projections. Our sub- personalities get hooked ... this is different from sharing from centre. In an interchange if we get an emotional charge, that energy is ours and not the other person's. In subpersonality you identify with your feelings. We can also share from centre however. Then we aren't attached to it, we are simply observing. There is no charge on it.
>
> - Psychosynthesis group leader

We are now in a better position to understand the Psychosynthesis member who claimed he needed 'less protection'. It is the rule of such groups that in order to develop one must share: "The process in this group is unfolding: each one of us has the responsibility to share where we are." The individual member is also hungry to 'get closer to people'. However, he is told explicitly that if he doesn't share from 'centre', if he relates from personality or ego, if he identifies or gets attached, he is not only in danger but he

is dangerous. So the adherent tells himself 'don't feel' and
simply can't find the courage to share. For it is not only
what the group tells him about the dangers, the doctrine
expresses dangers he already feels. Ironically, the ego which
is felt to form a barrier against close encounters, on the one
hand, is a porous, leaky substance which conducts contamination, transforms 'sacred' energy into poison, and fails to
protect the individual from being drained and/or manipulated,
on the other.

In the remainder of this chapter, an attempt will be made
to determine more precisely what such fears express about the
relationship of individual and society. Are they part of the
desire for "better" or "closer" relations or another
expression of narcissism and the desire to escape community?
Why should such fears be expressed and what do they imply
about our society?

One of the most interesting aspects of such fears are
their primitive "contagion" quality. It is as if the
individual is seen as porous or leaky absorbing and trans-
mitting dangerous substances. Such fears, while not part of
accepted modern vocabulary, are recognizable as "pollution"
beliefs -- a phenomenon which has been extensively studied
and documented in other tribes and cultures. Some of the
most interesting theories concerning such beliefs have been
developed by the social anthropologist, Mary Douglas. Her
theory is that such fears are important clues to the nature
of social organization, norms and values of primitive
societies. In addition, she feels that as such fears are
universal they may be used to examine the relationship between
order and disorder, society and individual, in whatever
context they appear. Douglas has a commitment to developing
conceptual systems applicable to both sociological and
anthropological data. In carrying out this commitment, she
consistently works with Durkheim's concepts about the relation
of religion and society, as well as her own, and her theories
dovetail with our concerns in this chapter (Douglas, 1966,
1978).

Pollution Beliefs and Boundary Confusion:
Douglas' Theory of Purity and Danger

In Purity and Danger (1966), Douglas sought to
demonstrate that pollution and dirt, while differing in
substance for primitives and ourselves, do not differ in
function. Dirt or pollution, she states, is simply "matter
out of place." Any society's organization depends upon the
establishment of an intricate set of distinctions -- of
boundaries and lines which divide individuals, groups and
classes from each other and define the parameters of a given
society. These distinctions are governed by rules for social
behavior and determine right from wrong, order from disorder.
It is as if from the continuum of experience,social order is
established by process of selectivity -- social reality carved
out by ignoring some aspects of experience and highlighting
others. The ignored experience forms the dark interstices
between the social categories and allow these categories to
be visible. When these lines and categories are clear, matter
is "in place." When the margins or lines separating dark and
light become blurred, we may say that pollution has occurred.

This 'matter out of place' can be both symbolic and
real. For instance, Douglas describes how our notions of
domestic dirt have more to do with our systems of order than
with the reality of germs. Kitchen utensils in the bathroom,
or a toothbrush on the livingroom coffee table are seen as
'dirty', provoking a feeling of discomfort and even mild
danger, whereas they merely represent 'matter out of place'.
On the other hand, there are many situations in which the
matter out of place is invisible and/or symbolic. For
instance, people are seen as dangerous if in fact they
transgress the symbolic and sociological order of a society.
This is particularly true of transgressions which are not
covered by the moral codes or enforced by firm sanctions.

> People think of their own social environment as con-
> sisting of other people joined together or separated
> by lines which must be respected. Some of the lines
> are protected by firm physical sanctions .... But
> whenever the lines are precarious we find pollution
> ideas come to their support. (Douglas, 1966:165)

By crossing these lines a person becomes symbolically 'matter
out of place'. Those people passing from one group or

category to another because of marriage, death, birth, puberty,
etc. and are therefore temporarily marginal, are seen as
possible sources of pollution.

> Danger lies in transitional states, simply because
> transition is neither one state nor the next, it is
> undefinable. The person who must pass from one to
> another is himself in danger and emanates danger to
> others. The danger is controlled by ritual which
> precisely separates him from his old status, segre-
> gates him for a time and then publicly declares his
> entry to a new status. (Douglas, 1966:116)

Hence, when examining pollution beliefs from Douglas' view-
point, it is important to bear in mind that:

1. Pollution beliefs center on situations or things
   which threaten the social boundaries defined by
   a society.

2. People who are in themselves polluting are often
   those occupying the interstices between social
   categories, (marginal in Mary Douglas' terminology).

3. Pollution is dangerous both to the polluter and
   the polluted. (Another way of saying that
   marginal people are seen as both dangerous and
   endangered).

These points do not exhaust Douglas' notion of the attributes
of pollution, but they are particularly relevant to the "cult
of man" beliefs that we have been exploring. It is evident,
for instance, that the boundary seen as threatened is that
separating not one group from another but one individual from
another. This suggests that it is the lines or rules
governing the relation and separation of individual that are
experienced as unclear, poorly defined or in jeopardy. It
also suggests, in the sense that each individual is seen as
dangerous and endangered, that adherents are like people
passing through a "rite de passage," somehow in transition,
or stateless.

This last suggestion, however, seems an inadequate
explanation of the fears of "cult of man" adherents for two
reasons. Firstly, such groups are formed neither of deviants
nor of those undergoing a prolonged 'rite of passage' in any
traditional sense. Most members are adult by any measurement
and certainly not deviant in any overt sense. They are middle
to upper middle class, in their late twenties with well
defined occupational roles (Smith, 1975; Stone, 1976;

Wallis, 1977). There is no indication that at the end of
training members attain any status in the wider social sense
that they didn't have before. Despite the fact that trainees
are supposed to be "progressing" towards developing their full
potential and goals are clearly labelled and described by the
individual group, the experience seems to be one of endless
process.

Secondly, and more importantly perhaps, adherents of such
"transpersonal" training groups do not see only other members
as dangerous and endangered; they see all people to be in this
state. For such individuals, society appears to be made up of
a collection of people all in transitional states.

This seems an impossible and confusing image in the
context of the anthropological notions of transition and
transgression in the small, stable society of the primitive
tribe. In order to interpret the contemporary fears of the
members, we need a modern equivalent to describe the relation
of individual and social order, purity and danger. Such an
equivalent is to be found in a socio-psychological theory of
Erving Goffman.

A Socio-Psychological Alternative: Goffman's "Face-Work"

One of the best descriptions of the rules and lines
separating and defining individuals is presented by Goffman's
work on "face-work" (Goffman, 1967:5-46). "Face-work" as a
concept fits nicely into Mary Douglas' discussion of social
lines and categories because it contains both a notion of
inner identity (which may be seen as stemming from a sense of
belonging to a group) and a notion of surface interaction,
defined by social rules or etiquette.

In the latter context, Goffman defines face as "an image
of self delineated in terms of approved social attributes"
(Ibid.:5). It is not something located in the individual but
constructed in the flow of social interaction existing between
individuals. People are dependent on others to support,
verify and acknowledge their 'face'. If proper 'face' is
maintained participants are seldom conscious of the process
of face-work, but if 'face' is questioned or destroyed, it can
cause embarrassment and hurt; people in fact become emotionally
attached to a given image and feel destroyed if it is

destroyed. Hence, people who do not know how to support or save other people's 'face' are seen as dangerous. Similarly, people who participate in situations without proper 'face' -- the ready line expected of people in certain situations -- are "out of face." They are in the "wrong face" when they adopt a line which they cannot sustain. Such people are also a threat because others are then obliged either to witness his "loss of face" or to "give face" -- i.e. "arrange for another to take a better line than he might otherwise be able to take."

It is evident that much of this kind of interaction is carried on in a formal context, having to do with social skills, etiquette and public behavior. In this sense what Goffman is describing is the intricate rules of give and take which allow people to relate to each other.

But for Goffman, the concept of 'face' also has a deeper connotation of identity as formed in a vital, particular relationship to another person. Goffman argues that when we say that someone is involved in or committed to someone else, we really mean that that person is involved and committed to maintaining the other's 'face'. It is as if in the process of intimacy the two parties decide upon, construct elaborate and maintain identities that are then dependent upon and grounded in, that particular relationship. The participants come to count upon these identities as real and attach deep emotions to them. It is in this sense that the 'sacred' nature of face that Goffman describes becomes apparent. Situations in which this aspect of face must be negotiated are experienced as questions of survival and therefore of considerable peril.

In sum, face-work involves social interaction, both of a public and an intimate nature. It describes and determines the relationship between self and others. It is a fragile and contextual process, particularly vulnerable to rapid social change (Yai-fai Ho, 1975) and yet expressive of it. We have coined the term "facelessness" to describe the result of the breakdown of the process of face-work.

Returning to Mary Douglas' notion of the relationship between social 'state' and pollution, it may be argued that primitive state and modern face are equivalent on many points.

Moving from face to face is imbued with all the dangers
associated with moving from state to state in primitive
tribes. Both are images with which the individual identifies,
composed of a role, a line, or attitude adopted by the
individual playing a role and requiring the support of other
people to maintain. State seems a more permanent, face a
more ephemeral term for this image and indeed it would seem
that in stable societies the image is more solid and long-
lasting. In a stable society, one's identity is relatively
changeless. The role one plays, the image one has, the people
one knows, remain fairly constant -- identity is not being
continually tested and the rules for its maintenance are fairly
well understood by all participants in a given situation. In
these societies, an individual is required to change this
image only a few times -- and these were generally marked by
"rites de passages" -- one leaves childhood and becomes an
adult, one changes from single to married, to parent, etc.
Rites of passage are partly created to deal with the danger
those in transition present to others and to themselves.

     'Face', however, with its ephemeral implications, is much
better suited for our society. Increasingly, it may be
argued, criteria for public and private face-work are becoming
obscure. Each new contact we make requires anew the
establishment of 'face'. This requires arriving at a
consensus and an understanding.

> If a person is to employ his repertoire of face-saving
> practices, obviously he must first become aware of the
> interpretations that others may have placed upon his
> acts and the interpretations that he ought to place on
> theirs. (Goffman, 1967:13)

     While in a stable society, participants in a given
interaction can be expected to understand the rules; people in
a highly fluid society can be less relied upon to know the
appropriate context.

     This sort of contemporary difficulty can perhaps be
illustrated by the effects of changing dress codes. While
in the past dress codes were linked first to class, and within
class to activity, today's more relaxed codes have paradoxically resulted in dress becoming much more important as an
indicator of the 'face' of the dresser, both in a public and
private sense.

> When street clothes and stage costume come to
> be seen as having something to do with the body, they
> will also come to appear to have something to do with
> the character of the person wearing them. At that
> point this rule for marking oneself in a public
> milieu will go weirdly out of control: reading "more"
> into the appearance of strangers, men and women will
> have less of a sense of order in their perceptions of
> strangers. (Sennett, 1977:72)

Today, when dress is divorced not only from class distinctions but from distinctions of location (public vs.
private) and occasion, it is even more loaded in terms of what
it expresses about the 'inner' identity or 'sacred' face and
even less attached to social interaction in which both parties
are aware of the signals. This can perhaps be best
illustrated by the following anecdote:

A young woman meets a young man at a lecture. She is
introduced by a mutual friend and, while very drawn to him,
does not have long to talk. The next week the man calls and
asks her to a concert. She wants to impress him and is
therefore in some consternation about how to dress. The
event is no guide as she could wear anything from blue jeans
to an evening dress. She is aware, however, that whatever
she chooses will broadcast a great deal of information about
her 'lifestyle' and personal orientation. Her solution to
the dilemma is clever: she dresses in a conservative skirt
and blouse and sits down to wait. When the young man arrives
at the door dressed in blue jeans, she asks him to come in a
moment; she has just come home from work, she explains, and
will run up and change.

In this particular occurrence, interactional face-work
was made considerably more difficult by the breakdown in the
normative system of dress-codes. As a result, the young
woman had to take extra measures to prevent possible loss of
face and exposure which she would have felt if she had made
the wrong choice. Everyday contacts can become considerably
more dangerous and fraught with tension.

To complicate this situation, modern society presents us
with a situation in which we are expected to play not one
role but many, at times contradictory and/or competing. Each
one of these roles requires a different 'face' and involves us
in often quite different groups. With the breakdown between

public and private (Sennett, 1977) and the general erosion of interactional codes, however, these competing roles may easily be confused. People who confuse contexts, who overlap competing roles, are both dangerous and endangered, dangerous not only because they might cause others to lose 'face' but because they may be perceived as 'two-faced', holding simultaneously identities supportive and undermining of the other's 'face'.

With a clear internal sense of identity, such a variety of 'roles' may be easily mastered, but the roles themselves can no longer 'yield' a sense of identity. They are too transient, mobility too common, class and social barriers too easily penetrated (Luckmann and Berger, 1964; Wallis, 1977) and in addition, an awareness of roles as 'socially constructed', an awareness introduced into our culture but increasingly more popularized produces a kind of self-consciousness which makes identification difficult (Turner, 1976; Eister, 1972).

Even more important than the breakdown in the norms governing day-to-day interaction, is the threat to the deeper, more 'sacred' sense of face represented by the increasingly transient nature of personal commitments.

Weigert and Hastings (1977) have discussed this threat in terms of the increasing specialization of the family into the sole societal vehicle for identity construction and main- tenance. While the family has assumed greater and greater responsibility in this area, it is paradoxically less able to fulfill it. The family was always, by nature, transient; the identities it formed and supported dissolved inevitably by time and death. However, with the family growing continually smaller and the divorce rate rising, the potential for identity loss grows. In the meantime, as other institutions have evolved, rationalized and specialized, there is less and less capacity in society as a whole to support and legitimize identity loss.

Viewed in Goffman's terms, it may be said that prolonged support for another's 'face' implies commitment to that 'face', emotional and otherwise. One becomes attached to and comes to rely upon the other's image which one helps maintain. In situations where relationships cannot be counted upon to

remain stable, such involvement becomes dangerous -- support
for one's own face may be suddenly withdrawn, leaving one
emotionally exposed and at the mercy of unmasked passion. Or
the image, to which one has devoted energy in maintaining and
has become attached to, may disappear leaving one drained and
cheated.

In response to these uncertainties and complications of
modern face-work, face-work becomes perilous and 'faces' seem
thin and insubstantial and the desire is to abandon the whole
process both in terms of norms of social conduct and in terms
of identity (Turner, 1976; Weigert and Hastings, 1977).
However, and this is the beauty of Goffman's concept of face,
as the masks become more and more ephemeral, people paradoxically do not feel more "open," closer to others, more
authentic. This is because face-work is necessary for
relationships to exist. According to Goffman, the definition
of involvement is commitment to facework. In order for
people to relate, they must in fact be separate entities --
the margins both keep people separate and allow them to be
close.

In summary, we have suggested that the ambivalence which
the "cult of man" members experience concerning close personal
relations reflects the experience which members have of being
"between states," perpetually in a state of identity flux or
ambivalence which in primitive tribes was associated only with
passing through a rite de passage or with those who have
somehow slipped outside of the categories that define social
beings and their interactions. As the members are not
deviants or initiates in any traditional sense in terms of the
larger culture and as they see not only themselves but all
individuals as dangerous and endangered, we have attempted to
explain their fears in terms of a modern equivalent to
"statelessness" which we have termed, after Goffman,
"facelessness." This is the fear of interaction based on the
breakdown of interactional codes which define social interchange and the identity forming groups which provide the
deeper sense of identification. Such a fear is highly
ambivalent. It produces a sense of being endangered by
precisely the thing most desired. Loneliness grows greater to
the extent that relations are feared.

While such an explanation seems to fit the phenomena described, providing a solution to the seeming paradox of privatism and hunger for community present in the belief systems of these groups, it in turn raises an important question. If in fact the above is an accurate description of the experience of members in the society at large, why is it that all people are not attracted to "cult of man" groups? We may presume that in our highly diverse society the kinds of strains we have described are not distributed evenly and would not therefore produce the same anxieties in everyone. We must look, therefore, for particular characteristics in the individuals who join these movements which would make them more susceptible to the experience of 'facelessness'.

This question would be best answered in terms of large scale survey data on these groups which is, unfortunately, not available. However, one survey study on est has produced some interesting data in this context. This survey indicated that the mean age of est members was 35.11 years. 31.8% had no religious beliefs before joining the group. Over half (53.7%) had no children at all. 68% were single (as opposed to 50% of the general population) (Ornstein, 1975). This general picture of being unattached in terms of family or religion is supported by Stone's profile of human potential groups in general:

> Some of the life-style characteristics that appear to go along with participation in human potential groups are never having married, a recent change of address, and a tendency to join groups and try out new experiences. (Stone, 1976:107)

The composite picture suggests that members of these groups are even more likely than normal to experience 'facelessness' due to the breakdown of identity-forming groups and the subsequent transience of relationships.

Whether members of these movements are also more affected than average by the breakdown of interactional codes is more difficult to determine. However, it should be noted that these groups direct their advertising campaigns at two distinct occupational groups. The first are salesmen or small businessmen. This is particularly true of groups such as Silva Mind Control and est who make their pitch to salesmen suggesting that their programs will improve their members' business and sales capacities. The second occupational group appealed to by groups like Psychosynthesis and Arica are the helping professions: counsellors, social workers, ministers, teachers, etc. Psychosynthesis groups in particular see their programs as not only producing psychosynthesis in the students but training them in turn to counsel and help others.

It is impossible without a breakdown in terms of precise occupation to know if in fact it is these occupations which are attracted to the "cult of man" groups. The two, however, have an interesting feature in common. They are both what might be termed "high empathy" professions. By this is meant that they are professions which depend for their success on the ability of the individual to 'tune in' quickly and adequately to the identity of strangers or near strangers. Such occupational groups are more likely than average to be affected by the breakdown in interactional codes which make it easy to 'type' other people and so interact with them. For instance, fifty years ago if a man and a woman were approaching a door together both would expect the man to open the door. Today, if a man and a woman who don't know each other well approach the door this issue is not at all clear. Whether the man opens the door or waits for the woman to do so or vice versa will expose considerable information about personal orientation, without either person knowing how that information will be received by the other. This is a minor occurrence and one which in normal circumstances can be dismissed. But if in fact one or the other is trying to make a sale and the impression created can determine the success of his/her effort, such interactions become important.

In this context, one of the most outstanding demographic features of the est sample (and of human potential members in general according to Stone) as compared to the general population is that although they have a much higher level of education (40% have had graduate or professional training after college compared to 17% of the general population) their mean income is the same as the general population (Ornstein, 1975). Presuming that education is generally correlated with higher earning, it seems that adherents are not succeeding at their jobs as well as might be expected. In addition, the discrepancy between income and education might well create a status inconsistency which has been seen as "unfavourable for the consistency and stability of the self" -- that inner 'sacred' sense of face (Luckmann and Berger, 1964:335).

From the above description of the known attributes of "cult of man" members, a relative deprivation or compensatory argument could seem to be made. The members seem to be to some degree both socially and economically dislocated, if not deprived. However, for such an interpretation to be valid, it would also have to follow that the group itself provided the social bonds lacking, or the philosophical justification for economic deprivation. "Cult of man" groups do neither. As has been pointed out repeatedly in earlier chapters, such groups are extremely transitory. What community they offer is finite, fragile and short-lived. Nor do the groups reject the value system of the society at large. The "trainings" are orientated not so much towards providing alternate goals and values to those of the secular world, but towards finding better ways of achieving these goals. Success in economic activities and interpersonal relations figure heavily in members testimonials as to the merits of the "trainings" (Wallis, 1977; Stone, 1976; Tipton, 1977). It would seem that these groups act to express and affirm the condition of "facelessness," as opposed to trying to counteract it. Recognition of "facelessness" is the basis of a new way of life.

> Often a crisis in life deprives a person of the function
> or role with which he has identified; an athlete's body
> is maimed; a lover's beloved departs; a worker is fired
> or retires. Then the process of disidentification is
> forced on one and a solution can only come by a process
> of death and rebirth in which the person enters into a
> broader identity ...
>
>   - Roberto Assagioli, Psychosynthesis leader

In the next chapters, we will discuss at some length the rituals which are built on this recognition of facelessness. Here, we would like to give just one example of which the activities of the "cult of man" members seem to embody the dilemma of interpersonal relations in a "faceless" world.

A vivid expression of the way that intimacy seems to recede, the more it is pursued, is provided by the norm of direct eye contact which is held by all "cult of man" groups. This norm directs adherents to never simply glance at someone to whom they are talking, but instead, to gaze steadily and deeply into the eyes, even if that person is completely unknown. The idea behind this is that if 'real', intimate or 'authentic' contact is to be made, a superficial glance will not suffice. Considerable pressure is exerted to get members to overcome their nervousness at deep eye contact. All "cult of man" groups have rituals designed as a practice of prolonged staring into the eyes of randomly selected partners. It is implied that people who are unwilling to do this, are somehow shifty, superficial, dishonest, and not truly interested in getting close to others, but rather involved in their own egos or 'acts'.

Social psychologists, such as Goffman and Simmel have studied at some length the implications of eye contacts. Human beings in all societies have an elaborate code of eye contacts. Variations in terms of the length of contact, the directness of contact, the distance at time of contact, form an entire code of social distance and intimacy. The avoidance of eye contact is equally important, and in many cases, people who are not socially 'open' to each other are formally forbidden from any kind of prolonged eye contact. Some social undesirables are given a non-person status by ritual 'not-seeing' (Goffman, 1963:84). At the opposite extreme is the sense of absolute union which is sought by the "cult of man" member and which is commonly recognized as one of the powerful consequences of direct, prolonged eye contact.

> Of the special sense organs the eye has a uniquely sociological function. The union and interaction of individuals is based upon mutual glances. This is perhaps the most direct and purest reciprocity which exists anywhere ... so tenacious and subtle is this union that it can only be maintained by the shortest and straightest line between the eyes and even the smallest deviation from it, the slightest glance aside, completely destroys the unique character of this union. (Simmel, in Goffman, 1963:93)

However, as Goffman points out, the power and sociological meaning of the stare depends largely on its relationship to other kinds of eye-contacts. "The more

clearly individuals are obliged to refrain from staring
directly at others, the more effectively will they be able to
attach special significance to a stare" (Goffman, 1963:95).
If all taboos against staring are removed, and indeed all
nuances of glance forcibly eliminated, the prolonged stare in
fact becomes meaningless. If all people are public, the
invasion of privacy associated with staring is impossible.
But it was precisely the sense of invasion of privacy which
created the sense of unusual and intimate contact. As with
dress and language, once the vocabulary of glance is
eliminated, there can be no visual conversation and with no
conversation, no creation of face, which as we mentioned, is
an aspect not of the individuals but of their interaction.
Without face, there can be no involvement and without
involvement, no real sense of intimacy or contact. Intimacy
or closeness, hence, seems a by-product of the interaction
based on manipulation of separations and distinctions. If
pursued as an end in itself, it seems like the proverbial
will 'o the wisp, to retreat as its pursuer advances.

    This brings us to our concluding point. When Durkheim
suggested that the "cult of man" would be a result of the
diversity and specialization of society which would produce
a sense in individuals of having "nothing in common" with
other individuals, he was making an implicit comparison with
his notion of primitive society in which the religion
expressed what people had in common. In the unilineal kinship
system which he explored in Elementary Forms of Religious
Life, the things which people had in common were viewed as
twofold. Most basically, they had in common their kinship
group, linked by blood and symbolized by the totem. They
also shared the rules and rituals which governed their
individual relationship to the 'sacred' phenomena.

    While Durkheim did not spell out in detail what having
"nothing in common" would mean, we may, from this comparison,
presume that it would represent a disintegration of both these
systems: the groups with which a person identified and the
rules and rituals which governed interaction. In fact, as we
have discussed at some length, such a disintegration has been
recognized by social scientists as being a by-product of
diversity and specialization of the modern technological

world. Diversity and specialization would hence seem
conducive to creating a sense of universal "facelessness" akin
to the primitive feeling of "statelessness" when people seemed
adrift, outside of the boundaries which governed and ordered
those societies. Statelessness is in turn (according to
Douglas) linked to pollution fears, fears of interpersonal
contamination, because stateless people are 'matter out of
place'. And the belief which most strongly highlights the
problem of contamination, of the sacred by the profane, is
the one that locates them in the closest proximity: within
the single human individual. Hence, the notion of the
sacredness of the human individual with the accompanying preoccupation with pollution and contamination, is a vivid
symbolic expression of the social experience of "having
nothing in common."

Another way of expressing this is using Douglas' notion
that the human body is the symbol of society (Douglas, 1978).
If the major problem in that society is the breakdown of
social boundaries separating individuals, with resulting
interpersonal contamination, this can be symbolized by a body
in which sacred and profane are both equally present and in
danger of contaminating one another because the "distinction"
is not clear. The sacred-profane distinction is the most
fundamental and universal, according to Durkheim. Only in a
situation of great diversity do both the sacred and the
profane come to be represented in terms of the individual.
And the danger of contamination, which such intimacy of sacred
and profane is bound to create, is symbolic of the danger of
interpersonal confusion which occurs when diversity and
specialization break down notions of social boundaries and
rules.

It goes further, however. Durkheim suggested that the
"cult of man" would not only reflect "having nothing in
common," it would also be an expression of what men still had
in common. It would not only acknowledge in its beliefs and
rituals the breakdown of the bonds uniting men, it would
also proclaim new ones. The "cult of man" would still act to
empower, to motivate and restrict its members out of the
recognition and reaffirmation of their common humanity.

In this chapter, we have discussed the way in which the central conception of the sacred as lying within the single individual is linked inextricably to a preoccupation with personal and interpersonal contamination. Thus, despite avowals on the part of the groups that they are providing a chance to get closer to the world and other people, members and literature express a terror of interpersonal encounters. This terror we have interpreted as expressing the problems involved in having "nothing in common" in terms of identity and interaction. In the next chapter, we will discuss what, in the view of the groups and of Durkheim himself, is the positive aspects of this experience: the chance to "enter into a broader identity," that of a member of humanity idealized. In exploring these new bonds, this new sense of having something in common, we will look at the rituals of the "cult of man" groups. For it is in rituals, "the rules of conduct which prescribe how men should behave in relation to sacred things," that the new bonds which the "cult of man" groups offer their members will be embodied.

RITUALS IN THE "CULT OF MAN"

Ritual has been largely ignored in the sociology of religion, having come to be defined as an empty form of action divorced from the internal moods and motivations of the actor. As has been pointed out by social anthropologists, this leaves sociologists with no terminology to deal with "symbolic action (outward, ritual behavior) which correctly expresses the actor's internal state" (Douglas, 1978:20). This inarticulateness is particularly frustrating when attempting to study emerging forms of religious life where the ritual behavior is not only heartfelt by the individual who performs it, but also highly expressive of the group which aids in directing and shaping that behavior. Even when ritual is merely empty conformity, it still presents a problem of the relation of symbols to social life. But when the conformity is genuine, ritual offers an arena for exploring the relations between the individual and the group, the group and the symbol system in which it finds expression (Douglas, 1973:21).

In addition to this general consideration, it seems that the issue of ritual is particularly relevant to "cult of man" groups. It was noted in the last chapter, that for primitive tribes, individuals going through a change of state (and therefore dangerous and endangered) were protected by care-fully constructed rituals (Douglas, 1966). Perhaps because of the sensation which members have of being continually in flux, the "cult of man" groups are notable for the variety and number of ritual techniques. In some cases, the groups see themselves as in the business of ritual creation:

> At Arica, we teach the art of creating rituals and ceremonies, liturgies for the new spiritual consciousness.
>
> — Arica leader

Durkheim, in his discussion of Elementary Forms of the Religious Life, devoted a large section to rituals. He saw rituals as divided essentially into two groups which he termed the 'negative' and the 'positive' cult. He saw both

as being concerned with governing the relationship between
sacred and profane, society and the individual. The negative
cult concerns taboos and interdictions, keeping the sacred
and profane separate so as to prevent contamination. The
positive cult, on the other hand, governs the intercourse
between sacred and profane. The two are inseparable, however,
for unless the profane is somehow 'purified', interaction with
the sacred is impossible.

In the next chapters, we will take a closer look at the
specific rituals in the specific groups we have been
exploring. These rituals appear to fall into three groups.
On the one hand, there are the purification rituals which
clearly fall into the negative cult and flow from the beliefs
about pollution we have discussed. On the other, there are
the transformational rituals, which are positive rituals of
power and which seem closely linked to the 'cast of thousands'
beliefs. Somewhere in the middle are the rituals which seem
to flow from the faith in rational technology of science.
These rituals provide the best 'skill testing' arena as well
as sharing some aspects of both the positive and negative
cults. It should be noted that in any one of the six groups
in our "cult of man" sample, the emphasis on one type of
ritual may be greater or less, but that samples of all three
types exist in each group. In addition, a given ritual may
fulfill all three functions.

We will discuss each type of ritual in a separate
chapter, concluding with a chapter analyzing the privatistic
aspects of rituals in "cult of man" groups.

CHAPTER VIII

RITUALS OF PURIFICATION

The rituals of purification fall into three categories in "cult of man" groups, corresponding to three steps in the process of separating sacred from profane. These three steps may be termed Disassociation, Reorganization and Fortification.

1. Rituals of Disassociation

One of the first messages which the "cult of man" groups seem to want to get across to new members or trainees is that "you are not what or who you think you are." However, in accordance with the anti-rational and anti-explanatory bias we have outlined in an earlier chapter, this message is not communicated in intellectual terms but, rather experientially, in the form of ritual.

In some of these groups this first step in the purification process is handled in a brutal manner. The idea is that adherents will only let go of their preconceptions and of their notion of who they are through some kind of severe jolt, which shakes them from their complacent sense of identity and/or their ability to understand.

One of the best known examples of the more severe or "jolting" disassociation rituals is the est Tirade. Est begins their "training" with some fairly established techniques of undermining personal identity, such as confiscation of belongings, limitations on personal freedoms for food and bathroom breaks (Goffman, 1961, 1967) and failure to give explanations (questions concerning the reason for the limitations are met invariably by the answer "because it works"). After establishing these limitations in the introduction to the weekend, an instructor enters to begin the first ritual of The Tirade.

> He wasted no time in getting down to business. There were no introductions, no preliminaries, no niceties. He glowered at us and announced that we were all assholes .... A woman in front of me began to shake.
>   "You are an asshole," he repeated loudly. "You are a machine. Your life doesn't work. You're an

>asshole because you pretend it does." He paced from
>one end of the platform to the other, punctuating
>each staccato statement with a thrust of his arm.
>(Bry, 1976:72)

For estians, this initial experience of being told that
you are not what you seem, is then acted out by the students
themselves in other rituals. One of the most striking of
these is the Danger Process. In this process students are
seated in four long rows facing the stage. One row at a time
is randomly called to the front to stand on the stage and
face the audience. They are then told to make eye contact
with someone still seated in the audience. This proves
extremely traumatic for many, partially no doubt because of
the stated significance of this ritual act.

>The trainees at the front of the room look out into
>the sea of faces and begin to smile. The trainer
>starts screaming, "Cut your act. Quit smiling. It's
>costing you your life." Most of the smiles quickly
>vanish. A few diehards start to laugh. The trainer
>and other est staff march up to these people. The
>trainer screams, est staff do nothing but stand in
>front of a trainee and look directly in the eyes.
>Women start to cry. Men clench their fists and tense
>up. The staring continues on the part of the est
>staff. The trainer is yelling, "Let it all come up.
>Cut your 'act' and see what you've been doing to your
>life. You'd rather be right than alive. You're all
>goddamned fucking machines. Complete assholes.
>Nothing in your life works for you and you wonder why.
>Look what you are doing to yourselves. Standing up
>here smiling, for Christ sake. What's so goddamn
>funny? The fact that you're pissing your life away?
>(Greene, 1976:68-69)

The stated purpose of this process is, ironically, to learn
to "be with someone."

These two rituals, the verbal assault on identity and the
staring confrontation, are present in some form in all the
other "cult of man" groups. Scientology is equally violent in
its attack, using a ritual called 'Bull-baiting' which involves
people pairing off, one student "baiting" the other by
haranguing him or her, insulting, attacking and exposing all
weaknesses in a manner as merciless as possible. Scientology
also stages the staring ritual (which they term Confrontation)
in pairs ... the two people staring into each other's eyes
without moving for as long as possible (Malko, 1971:123).

Shakti's ritual, while equally extreme, is more subtle. It is called the Turn-off. Periodically, students who have been working with the group in exercises, rituals or meetings, are simply told harshly to go away, that they are "stupid, lazy, unimaginative." This can be very disorientating to the student who is attempting to enter into a kind of disciple-leader relationship with the group (Palmer, 1976:110).

The other three groups, Arica, Psychosynthesis and Silva Mind Control, are somewhat gentler but no less firm in their attempts to produce disassociation in their students.

Psychosynthesis introduces early the notion of sub-personalities and has a ritual called "Disidentification and Self-Identification" which involves a meditation on four different aphorisms, one referring to the mind, one to the emotions, one to the body and one to the social roles, but all following the same pattern:

I have emotions, but my self is not my emotions. I experience an endless variety of emotional states, frequently contradictory and always changing. My feelings may swing from love to hatred, from calm to anxiety, from joy to sorrow, and yet my essence -- my true self -- does not change. At times my emotions seem to control me, to take me over, but I can learn to direct and integrate them. Though a wave of fear or anger may threaten to submerge me, these temporary states will pass in time. I can rise above my negative feelings if I refuse to identify with them and do not allow them power over me. I can observe and understand my emotions, and gradually learn to direct and harmonize them. I have emotions, but my self is not my emotions.

- Psychosynthesis Instruction Manual

Silva Mind Control also uses affirmations and meditation. The group introduces early the term "cancel cancel," a verbal charm used to ward off "negative thinking." In the group's relaxation exercises, members repeat such phrases as "The only difference between a genius and an ordinary person is that a genius uses more of his mind and in a different way. You are now learning to use your mind in a different way." The emphasis here is on creating an awareness in the individual that not only is she different than she appears, but that she is _more_ than she appears.

Finally, Arica introduces a personality typing system to members' lives. Students are typed and grouped in terms of their primary fixation, such as planning, vengeance, indolence. Once grouped with others apparently of this same type, students must self-consciously act out this fixation. This has the effect of alienating the student from her customary behavior and roles which she has thought of as her identity.

The effect of all these rituals, whether severe or less severe, is to create the initial gap ... the awareness that the self that acts in the world is somehow an artificial self, that true self is an inner and yet unknown quantity. In Durkheimian terms, therefore, we may say that the first step has been taken to separate the sacred from the profane, in the form of making adherents aware that in fact there are differences between inner and outer self ... that outer self is somehow inferior or negative and that their personal problems have arisen in part from their confusion of the different parts of themselves and the resulting contamination or destruction of their inner 'true nature'.

At this point, however, the realization is vague and the adherents' notion of themselves yet unstructured ... it has merely been disturbed. The next step in the purification process is to begin a more detailed organization of this new inner space.

2. Rituals of Reorganization

One of the unusual things about all "cult of man" groups is their tendency to create an elaborate internal map in which psychic dimensions are viewed spatially. This is not so strange when reviewed in the present context of the attempt to separate sacred from profane. In all religions space is an important variable in establishing this dichotomy (Durkheim, 1961; Eliade, 1968). In the Christian faith, for example, the whole interior of the church is considered sacred space, but within that space elaborate distinctions are made between more or less sacred spots. In Durkheimian terms, the church is sacred because it represents the gathering place of the community (the true source of the experience of the sacred). It is interesting that when the sacred becomes internalized in the individual human being, the elaborate spatial divisions are made internally in the symbolic space of the inner human psyche.

Of all the groups Arica has what is the most complex set
of distinctions. It is a point of pride with the leaders.

> The Arica Theory says there is a psychic territory that
> can be measured exactly ... we now know that territory
> completely. We are not any longer in idealism. We
> know with precision and detail everything that is
> inside. We mean all. It is the first time this
> territory has been measured and with this we know all
> the possibilities for a human being. That is why we
> speak of a scientific method for spiritual realization,
> for making the journey with precise calculation, and
> for reducing the time of necessary work. (Ichazo,
> 1976:33)

To this end Arica establishes not only a series of levels
of consciousness to be attained, but these are also grouped
into nine "domains of consciousness" which include four scales
having nine steps each. A variety of rituals, individual and
group, including chanting, meditation, physical exercise and
interaction techniques are used to induce the experience of
these different spatial locations (Lilly, 1972; Smith, 1975).

Psychosynthesis comes closest to Arica in terms of the
number and complexities of divisions. They provide members
with a chart of the relationship of different aspects, from
personality to Higher Self which exist within each individual.
They also have a notion of levels or stages through which the
individual must travel to reach the Higher Self, although
these are not as complex or as carefully defined as in Arica.
In the "Who Am I" ritual, the subject is instructed to
conceptualize himself as a series of concentric circles and
to visualize the various layers in succession. He starts
with the outermost layer and proceeds toward the centre. He
is told that there are a definite but limited number of steps
in the process and that this number varies with the individual.
Most subjects appear to go through from 10 to 15 layers.

A second similarity (which we will discuss in the next
chapter) is that the outer layer, which Psychosynthesis
leaders claim symbolize the individual's conflicts and
defenses on the personal level, is often visualized in terms
of machinery. The inner layers, on the other hand, which are
seen as symbolic of the "supraconscious and the transpersonal
self" are typically represented as a sun, or fountain in which
the self merges.

Silva Mind Control, as we noted in an earlier chapter, divides the internal levels into four: beta, alpha, delta and theta, although they randomly talk about going "deeper and deeper" in the relaxation exercises (which depend on taking deep breaths and "counting down" from one to three and then from ten to one), and on going "deeper than you have ever gone before ... to deeper, healthier levels of mind," which suggests uncharted areas.

Shakti, Scientology and est are not as precise about the different compartments of the inner space. Shakti believes that the nervous system and internal organization form pathways along which the "Being" may grow. To this end they spend considerable time in what is termed the "White Room Training" consisting of some "intellectual" work and "drawing geometrical diagrams." Est uses various meditation exercises, particularly one called the "Truth Process." This process begins with a relaxation or meditation exercise in which the individual concentrates on each part of the body in turn, following the instructions to "locate a space in your right foot," etc. He will then concentrate on some one problem that seems to be bothering him and "recreate the experience in a safe place." If the process gets too heavy the individual is supposed to "go to the beach," an imaginary spot of relaxation. Once "the truth" has been uncovered or experienced, it too is henceforth seen as a location in the spatial sense, a location deep within as opposed to the surface which is termed the "act" or "number."

> People are used to reacting in social settings and running their "numbers" on the people with whom they speak. Conversation with est graduates begins at an entirely different level. If an est graduate asks another how he is, he means it ... and the answer comes from Truth.
>
> - est graduate

In addition, est divides the mind into three levels of pain, 'pain level no. 1, 2, 3' to explain how people get cut off from reality and react in a preprogrammed machine-like way. Part of the Truth Process is to strip away these three levels to get at what is "real."

What reorganization rituals appear to do, therefore, is to begin a restructuring of the internal environment or

identity. In all cases this involves some further detailing
of the notion of surface vs. deep, artificial self vs. real
self, profane vs. sacred. The rituals are meant to help
adherents experience the nuances of the split between things
as they seem and things as they are and begin to create a new
identity to replace the one disturbed by disassociation
rituals. In Douglas' terms, it is also the beginning of the
construction of the lines and boundaries which create order
and prevent pollution. In this latter context, it is
interesting to note that those groups which have the most
complex and detailed reorganization schemes are those with
the most intense pollution fears, i.e. Arica and Psychosynthesis. It would appear that the greater the fear of
pollution, the more the need for boundaries and lines to
order all space. However, all these groups, as we have noted,
have pollution fears and all make some attempt at creating or
naming through ritual the internal lines which separate the
sacred from the profane. Finally, all groups describe
ritually an innermost "holy of holies" and spend some time at
fortifying and strengthening the barriers which separate this
spot from all others.

3. Rituals of Fortification

One of the most notable rituals shared by all "cult of
man" groups is the construction of an inner 'safe place'.
This ritual usually occurs towards the end of the training
and it is an elaborate and imaginative one. The ritual in
Arica (where the spot is termed the 'psychic space') est (the
'safe place') and Silva Mind Control (the 'lab') are all very
similar.

In Silva Mind Control, the ritual construction of the lab
occurs in the last weekend of the course and takes up the
better part of the afternoon. Some of the rituals leading up
to the course have made use of the "mental screen" of the
mind to practice precise, imaginative visualization. Now
this ritual training is used to construct something that
adherents can "take with them" when they graduate from the
course: the internal laboratory."

As is the case with all the visualization exercises, this
ritual begins by the relaxation, countdown technique. The

construction then proceeds as follows:

> Having counted down to level and assuming a relaxed
> state (most students were lying on the floor at this
> point) we were told that we were about to perform
> the most complicated exercise of the day: the lab.
> We were to choose any spot we wanted "from the bottom
> of the ocean to the top of a mountain, from a planet
> to a drop of water" in which to construct a room. In
> it, on shelves, we were to place any medicines and
> diagnostic tools we might need to diagnose and cure
> illness ... these could be real herbs or medicines or
> imaginary ones ... but we were to visualize them pre-
> cisely. We were to furnish the room ... placing doors
> and windows where we wanted. But we were to leave the
> south wall blank. We were to have a table with a
> clock that measured off not only hours and days but
> even years and centuries, and that could go both back-
> ward and forward. We were given time to visualize
> each one of these things carefully. We were to have
> a control panel on the table which had a volume and
> intensity control. We were to have two files, one for
> male data and one for female data. And we each
> received two counsellors, one male and one female ...
> which were presented to us one at a time through a
> secret, sliding door in the wall. These counsellors
> were there to help us with our diagnosing and problem
> solving. We were told that the south wall was to be
> our "screen" on which we could project our "cases" or
> those people who were ill and meant to be diagnosed.

> — fieldnotes, Silva Mind Control meeting

Students in Silva Mind Control are told that they can go
to their lab any time they have a problem to solve, although
the emphasis is on the lab as a laboratory for performing
psychic healings. In contrast, the "safe place" or "centre"
of est is not specifically designated for non-medical healing
but "to deal with all that has been experienced and that will
be experienced in the future."

> Basically it is a room, structure or house which con-
> tains everything which the trainee would need to sur-
> vive and live happily. That means the trainee would
> have his favourite books and records and other
> inanimate objects. In his imagination, the trainee
> starts with the foundation, literally builds this
> structure with his hands. The trainer guides the
> trainees in terms of the centre so that it contains
> some very specific items. Among them is a special
> television screen and most important, a door, which
> the trainee operates and which allows people in and
> out of the centre. (Greene, 1976:91-92)

Arica's 'psychic space' is also used as a private spot
for solving problems with the help of two guides and for

"clarification of our psychic powers."

Psychosynthesis, while not creating a room in such great detail, does have its adherents create a Temple of Peace. The students, in a relaxed meditative state, are taken on an imaginary journey up a mountain, which they are asked to envision in detail (vegetation, landscape, smells, sounds, the feel of the air as they climb). At the top of this mountain is a Temple of Peace. It has two rooms in it: a kind of antechamber, called the Hall of Peace. It is here that adherents receive final purification:

> Let the peace and silence here fill each cell of your
> body. Let it permeate your heart and your mind.
> Drink deeply of the silence, and feel it wash away
> all your cares and agitation. Take whatever time you
> need to be completely filled with peace and silence.
> Know that you can return to this inner place of peace
> and silence whenever you wish. And now we will pre-
> pare ourselves to make our way to the inner sanctuary.
> - Psychosynthesis Instruction Sheet

After this purification the students are instructed to enter into the inner sanctuary, the "Sanctuary of the Sun." This corresponds with the innermost level described in the Who Am I exercise, but here we have it more firmly circum- scribed by the walls of a room. Within this room adherents are asked to visualize a shaft of light coming from a 'spiritual' sun, into which the individual merges, feels warmed and energized, and up which the individual ascends until he is drawn into the "heart of the sun." As he ascends he is asked to visualize the other members of the group ascending their own "shaft of light and that you will come together again in the sun." This sun is described as a 'home', as a place "of great peace and joy and love where you really belong, where you can realize the best within you." It is also the place where the individual is joined to the divine in all other members of the group:

> As you approach the Heart of the Sun, be aware of the
> other group members who are there with you. Experi-
> ence them as divine beings in search of their own
> light and try to meet them at this level.
> - Psychosynthesis Instruction Sheet

It is finally the spot where the Source of Wisdom dwells, a kind of oracle of which the individual can ask any question

and receive an answer. The ritual ends by taking the
adherents on the return journey back to earth where they are
asked to "feel that you are sharing with others what you have
received by allowing the energy to flow forth from you in
this way. You can make the gesture of Benediction physically
if you so desire." Adherents are told to feel that they can
return to this place "whenever they wish."

It is worth noting, in passing, the emphasis on
connection with others in these inner sanctuaries. Psychosynthesis gives the most vivid examples of this but the other
three groups all have entrances through which anyone and
everyone with whom an individual wants to interact or heal
may be summoned. In this place, or at this level, they see
themselves as psychically connected to everyone. Considering
again the Psychosynthesis example, it is fascinating to note
how this supports Durkheim's basic tenet that the "cult of
man" will produce the assertion that what men have in common
is their humanity, idealized, and that this will be held
sacred. We will pursue this point later in an ensuing
chapter. For the moment we return to our exploration of these
rituals in terms of their implications for the "negative" cult
and the process of purification which is of central concern to
these groups.

We have noted that the purification process begins with a
jolt which disassociates the individual from his normal
personality or profane self. It proceeds with a restructuring
of the inner space in terms of compartments and/or levels,
through which the individual may journey to the sacred centre,
his true Essence. In the rituals we have just discussed,
 which we have termed the Fortification rituals, the individual
arrives at the sacred centre and he imaginatively constructs a
temple, lab, space, or house, which has walls and furnishing
which is the dwelling place of the sacred. Here, the
individual is told he can feel safe, i.e. he is no longer
dangerous and endangered because indeed a firm barrier in the
shape of carefully imagined walls has been constructed to
prevent pollution, to keep the sacred from contamination by
the profane. This barrier clearly works as a fortification
and a separation. The construction of this fortress is
therefore the final step in the purification process.

In sum, we have discussed a series of three kinds of
rituals which seem to make up the purification process in the
"cult of man" groups. This is the negative cult, those
rituals which act to separate the sacred from the profane.
Before, however, turning to the other kinds of rituals, the
"positive" cult, we need to examine one other element of the
purification process, the problem of preventing interpersonal contamination. In the last chapter, we noted that
pollution is feared both within the individual, in the event
of mixing the profane and sacred parts but also generalized to
interpersonal relations, where the personalities or profane
"passions" of others are seen as dangerous and endangering.
The individual may feel that he has found a safe place at the
end of the training. But how is he prevented from endangering
others?

4. Interpersonal Purification:
The Mirror Effect

In this section of this chapter, we intend to depart from
our comparative perspective to look at the specific group
process of a specific development group in Psychosynthesis, in
order to explore the way in which the problem of pollution, of
merging and confusing of boundaries is dealt with in this
context. In our analysis to this point, we have looked at
three steps in the purification process of the individual.
These rituals are linked to each other and follow in the
described manner. However, each is only one element of the
ritual life. In some groups, such as Silva Mind Control, the
training process includes all three of these elements in the
prescribed order. However, in groups like Psychosynthesis
and Arica where the process of establishing, clarifying and
fortifying internal boundaries is seen to be a lengthy one,
the steps of the purification process may span several
"trainings." As we have noted, it is also these two groups
which offer the most complex system of internal mapping and
which are most concerned with the problem of interpersonal
pollution. This may be due to the exceptional amount of
interaction which occurs in these groups. Whatever the cause,
they make particularly good cases for studying how interpersonal purification is achieved or attempted.

A close look at the fieldnotes of ten consecutive meetings of one "training" group at Psychosynthesis (spanning the life of this particular group) reveals an interesting reversal of the individual purification process. Although the terms must be interpreted slightly differently it seems that the group moves from the fortification of barriers to the elaboration of space to a final disassociation.

In the first meeting of this particular Psychosynthesis group, the theme, if there was one, was the need for trust. This involved considerable discussion of barriers and the necessity of barriers and the fear of "getting hurt." The leader discussed the fact that every person had their own armour "in some its the intellect, in some its the emotions." She then delivered her somewhat ambiguous remark, quoted in an earlier chapter, that in fact it was every person's 'responsibility' to share, i.e. to overcome the barrier, but that didn't mean that people should "unload their stuff" on other people. Then, one male member of the group reasserted the need for the barrier: "I would like to be with people right now and not feel like I have to fight them but right now I do feel I have to fight them." He challenged the group in general to a wrestling match. One of the other young men responded and they began to wrestle. The second man was clearly the better wrestler and won easily. Then ensued the following verbal exchange:

> Jack: It felt really good to me. He's stronger than me but it felt good when I realized that he wasn't going to hurt me. A clean fight always feels good, but a dirty fight doesn't. I feel fine. I feel initiated.

> Bill: I felt it was a terrific cleansing force. I feel incredibly clean.
>
> — Psychosynthesis fieldnotes

The group leader summed it up by the aphorism: "Trust is knowing your boundaries."

It is clear that this meeting was about reaffirming and fortifying boundaries. They were verbally recognized and the separateness of individuals symbolically acted out by a fight. When both men realized that it was going to be a 'clean' fight (a nice term from the point of view of Douglas' theories for an orderly fight which progresses according to rules) both men felt cleansed and purified, and, interestingly enough, initiated. It was as if the lines had been drawn and respected and therefore interaction could begin.

In ensuing meetings this interaction grew more and more intense, and as predicted in the first meeting, this involved the breakdown of barriers. It also involved an ordering of the group space. For instance, in the second meeting, there was considerable use of feeding and eating imagery, and the idea that some people were going to feed and some to eat. There was also recognition that some people shared easily while some were very withdrawn. In short, roles were recognized.

The space of the room began to be ordered as well. People sat in a circle around the edges of the room and someone who wanted to "act out" their emotional state would have to go into the middle. This centre was also referred to in gastronomic terms as the 'pot' as in "does anyone have anything to throw into the pot" (a statement the leader repeatedly made in order to encourage people to share). There was a sacrificial/communal aspect to the people who went into the centre to share. It was talked about as a dangerous act and something that someone did "for the group." People would come very 'undone' and emotional in the middle, while the others would sit around in silence, except for the leader who would continue to guide and question. (One is tempted to use the term 'grill': there are symbolic overtones of cannibalism similar to the Christian communion service in these rituals, as the "sharing" individual goes into the pot physically and unloads). After the first three cases of people 'acting out' (which included the fight and two cases of tearful confessions in the middle) there were instances on two consecutive weekly meetings of people symbolically breaking down barriers. In each of these cases, a woman (overtly claiming to be trying to work out problems of a feeling of oppression on the one hand, and strength testing on the other) got into the middle surrounded by the pillows. The woman would then fight her way out of this circle of pillows and physically tussle with other members of the group.

At the same time, a lot of physical interaction between group members began. At quieter moments, group members would lie in a circle with their feet touching and think of images such as the petals of a flower or the spokes of a wheel. At other times, they would stand with their arms around each other in a circle and suggest they were like parts of the sea anemone.

What seemed to be happening both in terms of the rituals and in terms of the images is that members saw themselves as separate but connected. Barriers are broken down (in terms of the pillows) but fights ensue (we are still separate). The images are of separate aspects of a single organism. This is a transitory state similar to that reorganization stage of the purification process of the individual. The distinctions are recognized but melt.

Such a sense of coming together, of becoming a part of a group, of interrelatedness is the expected pattern in most groups and would seem to reflect the express desire to feel "closer" to people. Close, but not too close. The theme of "not unloading" of not getting hooked, or "reowning projections" was reiterated as a commentary on group inter-action (by the group leader) and in discrete rituals in the group process. Nonetheless, this caution alone was not enough to counteract the growing involvement.

Then, in the last two meetings, an unexpected twist occurred. In the second to last meeting, the leader announced that the meeting would be spent discussing the 'norms' of the group, those unwritten laws which members were all acting out. Otherwise, she explained, we stop growing; become crystallized. The message was clear, "Things are not as they seem." Members were not going to be allowed to merge into blissful unawareness of group life. There was considerable resistance on the part of individual members to this discussion, but the leader won out. Suddenly, the group interaction which had seemed so 'real' and 'meaningful' was seen as an 'act' which must be disrupted if the individual members were to continue growing.

In the last meeting this disassociation was acted out. The group was dissolved ... a new gap created between the real self and the self that had acted in the group. In the interaction in the last session of the group this shift was

very marked. The leader began a movement exercise (no
talking) to the music of Bolero. The individuals linked up
into chains spontaneously moving to the music. Then as the
music seemed to get more pronounced, the movement becomes
increasingly hostile and aggressive. Instead of swinging
arms back and forth, people began to strike and hit each other
with their joined hands. They began to push people around and
throw pillows on top of them. Even after the music had
stopped, some individuals kept hitting each other with
pillows. The leader's comment was: "Wow, look at all these
dynamics coming out." People talked about meeting for a
party the next week but enthusiasm was low. People talked
about what they "got out of the group." The meeting and the
group ended.

In summary, the process of purification seemed to take
place in three steps, but like a mirror image of the
individual process. Initially, barriers were acknowledged
and fortified. People felt pure, but they were anxious to be
closer. As they became closer, pollution anxieties were
evident, but the boundaries were seen as joining them into a
system instead of merely separating them. Then as the
individuals appeared to be merging into the group, the leader
introduced the "jolt" that things were not as they seemed;
this wasn't real. Sure enough in the next meeting the system
seemed to run amuck, the interconnecting parts broke down and
new "dynamics" emerged. And the group broke up altogether.

Whether a similar pattern exists in all Psychosynthesis
groups or whether it is duplicated in other "cult of man"
groups, such as Arica, cannot be established without more
detailed fieldnotes. However, there is a kind of symbolic
logic about the above group process which makes one suspect
that such dynamics are far from uncommon.

What the Psychosynthesis member takes away from the group
is only her own growth, the extent to which she has achieved
the internal reorganization and purification described in the
individual process. Her interaction with others may have
helped her to reclaim projections, to achieve or recognize
different internal levels. The degree to which she will feel
comfortable leaving the intense interaction of the group will,
to a large extent, depend on the degree to which she has

developed a "safe," internal place which allows for a sense of
self-sufficiency as well as a sense, on a psychic or mystical
plane of being connected to all humanity. If such internal
progress has not been made, then the individual will feel
compelled to return to the group, to take another course, work
on more rituals to gain an internal sense of safety. In this
sense, the entire group process may be seen as a ritual of
disassociation, recapitulating the disassociation experienced
in the larger society of recurrent loss of identity groups
and breakdown of rules. The individual comes to the group to
practice over and over again, until she can handle it, the
experience of being disassociated and cut adrift. Mastery of
this experience depends on success at the internal ordering
and fortifying rituals. This is perhaps most poignantly
expressed by the Shakti ritual of the Mala Training:

> Mala and Lama, or Instructor and Student are isolated
> in separate rooms of the starship or hermitage,
> linked via intercom and video. They converse. Lama
> answers questions, performs tasks. Communication is
> cut off slowly, one way. Eventually Lama is left
> alone in a white, bare room. The goal of this
> technique is for the student to internalize his
> instructor, to be his own authority. To discover
> self, apart from senses, relationships. (Palmer,
> 1976:83)

The only way to prevent interpersonal contamination, it
would seem, is to eliminate attempts at interacting on the
profane level, to withdraw to the inner reaches where there
is safety and mystic reunion, to continue the external contact
only as an impersonal machine.

In the next chapters, which examine the rituals of the
"positive cult" governing the interaction between sacred and
profane, we will explore the felt advantages or powers that
accrue from this rather dismal picture of the possibilities
of interpersonal interaction.

CHAPTER IX

THE PERSONALITY AS MACHINE:
RITUALS OF MANIPULATION

This chapter will address itself to those rituals which
flow from the compromise between faith and science, and the
resulting belief in technology, precision and efficiency
discussed in Chapters V and VI. In those chapters, we
suggested that the problem of compromising the secular and
the sacred, whether in terms of science and religion or in
terms of economic organization, has historically proved
difficult for new religious movements. It was suggested that
the "cult of man" groups' apparent ability to effect such a
compromise was grounded in their unique view of the sacred.
As the line separating sacred and profane lay within each
individual as opposed to at the periphery of the group or
around consecrated ground, elements of profane society could
be admitted into the group structure and beliefs without fear
of contamination. In short, the problem of purity in the
"cult of man" groups is an individual as opposed to group
problem.

The problem is handled, as discussed in Chapters VII and
VIII, by disidentification with the outer 'profane' self.
Emotional involvement and attachment is withdrawn from the
outer personality and relocated in the inner Self. The outer
personality, empty of passion, is viewed as part and parcel of
the profane, outer world, and like that world, is viewed as
mechanical, rationalized, artificial and inanimate. As with
the sectarians, "cult of man" adherents are "in this world
but not of it," but for them "this world" includes their own
outer selves or personalities. This is nicely illustrated by
the following comment made by a Psychosynthesis leader when
discussing the ritual of the Levels (see Chapter VIII): "It
is a sad comment on our society, that the outer layer of the
self is frequently an image of machinery ... beneath this
layer ... a naked man, who is jailed, as it were by the
machines."

The choice of machine images to express the outer self/outer world is prevalent in all "cult of man" groups. This seems to some extent to be a reflection of, and reaction to, the concrete, machine-run world of the modern urban environment from which most members are recruited. The other source of such images seems to be, ironically, the social sciences. Glock (1976) has noted that the crisis in the sixties was in part due to the fact that the popularization of the social sciences led people to feel that reality was shaped neither by God nor the individual alone, but by a convergence of a number of social, psychological, biological and economic factors, impossible to sort out or control. Eister (1975) has suggested that the effect of the social sciences has been to create a normative dislocation through producing a widespread awareness of the relativity of all norms. Both these theorists, and others who have discussed the relationship of science and religion in the seventies, have viewed the new religious movements as an alternative to this demoralizing situation.

Durkheim, on the other hand, foresaw the relationship quite differently. As discussed in the first chapter of this dissertation, Durkheim expected that as the social sciences gathered interpretive power, they would eventually take over the representational aspect of religion which had functioned to explain society to its members. The relationship would be an uneasy one, faith tending to "anticipate science and complete it prematurely" and science tending to criticize and control faith, but the relationship would continue to exist.

In "cult of man" groups, the awareness of society as acting on the individual has produced an image of social interaction as mechanized and artificial, social responses and roles as prepatterned and predictable. It is all an "act" which has nothing to do with the real self, but which, none-theless, imprisons the individual and rules that self, and in which the personality plays a role. The famous est maxim that "you would rather be right than alive" expresses the inanimate, 'dead' quality of such preprogrammed performances.

No one ever stays with you because you are so busy running your goddamn 'act', you don't even have time

to notice that life is passing you by. You're a
perfect example of an asshole, a fucking <u>machine</u>.

- est trainer

But, true to Durkheim's notion, the "cult of man"
adherent does not seek solely to escape from this 'mechanical'
situation by finding refuge in a new spirituality or by
overcoming the mechanical 'programs'. The compromise between
faith and science in group beliefs results in a faith in, not
a rejection of, technology, precision and efficiency. For
the "cult of man" groups, the machine-like nature of the
outer personality, the body, the rational mind and the social
interactions in which these parts of the self participate,
are a given, irrefutable fact of reality. <u>The goal of the
"cult of man" member is not to interpret this reality any
differently in order to escape the machine</u>. <u>Instead, he seeks
to learn to manipulate the machine, to be the puppet master
instead of the puppet</u>.

For example, while the notion that man is a machine is
one of the first introduced to the est trainee (by way of a
jolt) it is also the last introduced, by way of 'getting it',
the point of the entire training process. On the last day of
the class, the trainer tells his trainees he is now going to
tell them "the secret of life." After a terrific build-up,
he announces that:

> Enlightenment is nothing more than realizing that you
> are a machine ... that's it, you're machines. Nothing
> but machines and you've got to accept it. Come from a
> position of being a machine. You'll work from cause,
> not from effect. (Greene, 1976:93)

The interesting thing about the machine image is in fact
its dual nature: a man can only be jailed by the machines
around him as long as he doesn't have his hand on the switch
or isn't pushing the buttons himself. If he 'causes' the
machine to run then he can use it to his own advantage.

This is illustrated by the Psychosynthesis ritual of The
Robot (as distinct from the Shakti ritual of the same name
which will be discussed below). The students are asked to
play at being robots without expression, thought or feeling.
They are then asked to feel that they are "really a human
being -- trapped inside a robot." They play out this human

side by moving, touching and expressing "freely." It would appear that the goal of the Psychosynthesis ritual is to "break out" of the machine except for the final instruction, "When you open your eyes, you may put on your everyday mask again. But remember that it is a mask and that there is a place within where you are pure being and pure love."

Purification rituals in the "cult of man" groups are aimed at bringing to the attention of adherents that they are machines. Once this is accomplished, however, other rituals are orientated not towards breaking down the machine but in learning to use it efficiently and effectively. These rituals may be broken into four groups: rituals of efficiency, rituals of communication, rituals of obedience and rituals of imitation. All four of these rituals help to maintain the "machine" in top working condition, with the end result that it may be manipulated to achieve the desired ends.

Rituals of Efficiency

These rituals are extremely pragmatic and straightforward "techniques," developed and practiced regularly in order to program the "machine" to perform habitual operations precisely and efficiently. The best examples of such rituals are found in est and Silva Mind Control. An example is the "Sleep Control" technique, taught by both groups:

> Sleep Control, a formula-type technique that you can use to enter normal, natural, physiologic sleep anytime, anywhere, without the use of drugs ... visualize a blackboard. Mentally have a chalk in one hand and an eraser in the other. Next mentally draw a large circle on the blackboard. Write a big X within the circle. Proceed to mentally erase the X from within the circle starting at the center, being careful not to erase the circle in the least. Once you erase the X from within the circle, to the right and outside of the circle, write the word deeper. Every time you write the word deeper you will enter a deeper, healthier level of mind in the direction of normal, natural, healthy sleep. Next write a big number 100 within the circle. Proceed to mentally erase the number 100 ... being careful not to erase the circle, and go over the word 'deeper' (this ritual is repeated over and over counting down from 100 to 1 until the person sleeps).
> — Silva Mind Control Instruction Manual

Similar techniques are used to train the "machine" self to lose or gain weight, wake up on time, control pain, develop

memory, control headaches, remember dreams, and solve
problems. Most of these, it should be noted, have to do with
aspects of the biological or physical self, which if not
properly regulated interfere with the smooth working of the
entire person.

The Arica emphasis on physical exercises is based on
this same principle. All members going through the forty-day
training are expected to exercise vigourously, daily.

> Poor physical shape means that we have not been getting
> sufficient exercise every day to keep the bio-computer
> in a controllable, quiescent, bland state at the high
> energy level. In poor physical shape, there are
> impulses not under one's control that make one rest-
> less. One moves about and does aimless kinds of
> actions with unknown desires taking the stage at
> awkward times .... One's 48 (that state of conscious-
> ness in which one is operating his human bio-computer
> completely rationally, without either positive or
> negative emotion) becomes more integrated, more
> unitized and more of one's available bio-computer is
> utilized. (Lilly, 1972:175)

Some of these, such as the problem-solving techniques,
would seem on the surface to be dealing with more complex,
less pragmatic issues. However, a look at such a ritual
suggests that 'problems' like all aspects of day to day
routine, are seen as mechanical misfunctions, which should be
corrected, not by mental problem-solving, but by mechanical
technique.

> Whenever you are ready to go to sleep, select any one
> problem you would like to solve; then get a water
> glass and fill it with water. And while you are
> drinking approximately half of the water, turn your
> eyes slightly upward and mentally say to yourself:
> "This is all I need to do to find the solution to the
> problem I have in mind." You will then put away the
> remaining half glass of water so that you may drink
> it first thing in the morning; after this you will go
> to bed and go to sleep. First thing in the morning
> drink the remaining half glass of water, turning your
> eyes slightly upward and mentally saying to yourself:
> "This is all I need to do to find the solution to the
> problem I have in mind." And this is so.

- Silva Mind Control Manual

Adherents who are taught this technique are told that it
is not important to determine how the problem will be solved,
merely to know that it will be.

This emphasis on method, even without comprehension or reason, of course is based on the idea of the outer personality as inanimate, a machine. Machines are not given reasons, they do not need explanations. They are incapable, in addition, of irrational mistakes. The rituals we will consider next, both those of communication (including those of duplication) are designed to eliminate, or at lease reduce, the margin of performance error.

Rituals of Communication

Many of the machine images used particularly for those outer personality aspects of rational thought, are borrowed from the computer. Arica talks about "metaprogramming" and the human "biocomputer" (a phrase coined by Lilly). Shakti talks about encoding and decoding, processing information. Silva Mind Control talks about "canceling" and Psychosynthesis, about "programs." The choice of the computer is undoubtedly an apt image for describing those rational thought processes which these groups see as part of the "ego" and therefore somewhat mechanical. Secondly, it is a good image for expressing thought processes uninhibited by irrationalities, such as human emotion, and therefore functioning efficiently as intended ('unclouded' by passions). Finally, however, it is an image which "cult of man" groups use to talk about human communication, because the computer absorbs 'raw data' in the forms of signs, words and symbols, processes this data and puts out a response also in signs, words and symbols.

It is worth noting, in passing, that the image of interpersonal relations which is created is one of 'dispassionate' communication for the sake of conveying information, but not for conveying emotion or feeling. This view of communication seems to flow directly from the attitude noted at the end of the last chapter, that interaction coupled with emotions is dangerous, and that real contact with others is possible only on the higher more mystical levels of the Real Self. Once divorced from emotion, however, interpersonal communication has one unexpected advantage. It can be precise, economical and efficient. The communications rituals in these groups are orientated toward this end. Take, for instance, the ritual in Shakti termed The Robot:

> The student plays a robot. The operator communicates
> in stylized format -- "Are you receiving me?", and
> gives commands in increments. Malfunctions in the
> robot are handled by repeating a command or starting
> at the beginning of the communication. (Palmer,
> 1976:84)

The purpose of this ritual is, among other things, "to
learn to communicate efficiently, patiently, precisely,
without emotive overtones." It is modelled after a
Scientology ritual called Termination, in which the student
practices "owning" a phrase, while his partner receives it,
acknowledges it and thanks him thus completing a "cycle" of
communication. In est, trainers often respond to comments
with "Thank you, I received that."

In addition, both Shakti and Scientology have rituals
which practice "processing" information. In Scientology, this
is called Dear Alice, and involves reading aloud and para-
phrasing. In Shakti, when an error is made, the page must be
repeated. Similarly, in all classes of Scientology, if a
student questions what is being taught it is presumed he
hasn't 'received' the communication, that there has been some
kind of mechanical breakdown in the process and the same
message is therefore simply repeated over and over until the
student appears to "get it."

Psychosynthesis has special Auditory Rituals for
developing acute auditory receptivity, practicing receiving
and cataloguing precisely auditory information.

Signs, of course, are not purely verbal. "Cult of man"
members also learn to receive visual information in a precise
way. As the only way that feedback can be created in a visual
situation is by imitation, these rituals focus on people
working in pairs, attempting precise duplication of each
other's activities. Shakti, Scientology, Arica, Psychosynthesis all have a ritual similar to the one described here:

> Two students stand facing each other. One leads and
> his partner mirrors his gestures. Two students sit
> on knees facing each other. At the snap of the
> leader's fingers, they rise simultaneously and say,
> "I I I" and sit. This is repeated with "you you you,"
> and "God God God." (Palmer, 1976:83)

This last ritual underlines the double nature of most of
the manipulation rituals we have discussed in this chapter.

It seems that to be capable of machine-like behavior on the
surface, precise and efficient, is intimately connected to the
sense of inner mystical self, wherein one is joined to
everyone and to the sacred. As pointed out in the last
chapter, the explanation of this connection lies in the
internal nature of the sacred and profane split. To build an
internal holy spot and to take refuge behind its barricades,
is to vacate the outer profane personality. One does not
abandon the personality, however, but employs the complicated
equipment with which the lab is furnished (see Chapter VII)
to run the external operations by remote control. In this
sense, rituals of manipulation are part of the positive cult,
regulating the interchange between sacred and profane. In
the above ritual, the profane selves of the two students
perform mechanical mirror exercises. This enables them,
however, to truly unite on the level of the sacred (hence the
repetition of the "I I I, you you you, God God God"). This
interchange is only possible if the external self is
neutralized so that contamination will not occur.
Manipulation rituals, in this respect, are also part of the
negative cult.

A third and final kind of precise and mechanical
communication is the notion of being able to carry out orders
(like a robot). This aspect is separated out for specific
attention in the next set of rituals.

Rituals of Obedience

In an attitude similar to making the best of a bad
situation, "cult of man" groups feel that if the individual is
a surface machine, at least he should have all the benefits of
that machine. He should be able to perform routine tasks
absolutely precisely and without error. There is considerable
emphasis, therefore, on being able to carry out orders. The
rituals which seem orientated toward developing this ability,
I have termed rituals of obedience.

Most obedience rituals consist of the minute observance
of monotonous instructions. For example, on graduating from
the course, est trainees may volunteer to help out at
subsequent est trainings. This is considered advanced
training obedience. The volunteers are set to do over and

over highly repetitive tasks, such as lining up chairs, in an
extremely precise manner (so that a thread stretched from one
end of the row to the other would be perfectly straight).
Carrying out the instructions is taken very seriously.

> My assignment was to cover several long, rectangu-
> lar tables with tablecloths. My instructions: each
> tablecloth was to be pinned with a square corner and
> should almost, but not quite touch the floor. Another
> mindless task. While I went through the motions I
> eavesdropped on a conversation a few feet away. A
> mistake.
> I looked up to see the person supervising the
> assistants standing alongside me. Confronting me with
> the directness characteristic of est-ers (a graduate
> can be known by his direct eye contact), he kindly but
> firmly instructed me to do the tablecloth over. "It
> touches the floor," he explained with a solemnity that
> from someone else would have indicated a critical error
> in a major undertaking. But there was no cruelty, no
> satisfaction, no judgement in his statement. It simply
> was. (Bry, 1976:101-2)

In Shakti and Scientology, the Dear Alice and the Robot
exercises also help to develop obedience. In Arica, an
exercise termed "I Hear and I Obey" combines breathing and
slow walking with repetition of the phrase "I hear and I
obey." (Women are given this ritual to perform more often
than men as Ichazo claims that they "have a hard time
listening" (Lilly, 1972). In all groups such rituals develop
a sense of self-consciousness about minute interactions.

Such training in obedience and precision has its
benefits. For one thing, it is excellent practice for modern
bureaucracies. It is claimed by est, for instance, that
graduates are "in great demand on the California job market.
A number of businesses, in fact, were reported to be hiring
only est-ers" (Ibid.:105). Glowing reports of the cheerful
and thorough on-the-job performance of est graduates are
repeated gleefully.

Such training also has benefits for the internal
authority structures of the groups. As much of ritual
activity of "cult of man" groups is internal and private
(particularly those rituals to be discussed in the next
chapter) it is difficult to evaluate the performance of
students. Performance is important, however, because of the
problem of authority in groups where the sacred lies within

each individual. This problem was noted by Durkheim in his
article on "cult of man" (1969). There he suggested that its
solution would be authority based on skill. This seems to be
true in "cult of man" groups, particularly those like
Psychosynthesis, Arica and Scientology which have an elaborate
gradation of courses. Students are evaluated (ironically) not
on their internal experience (which is invisible and to a
degree deemed inexpressible) but on their external performance
(their ability for dispassionate and exact interchanges,
physical control and obedience to instructions). The logic
behind this, in group terms, is that controlled external
performance signals that disidentification has occurred. As
this is an essential criterion for the development of the
inner, sacred self, it is considered a good indicator of
spiritual progress. That these external 'skills' are linked
to authority patterns is witnessed by the fact that it is
those people who graduate from the top level courses who are
admired and who become licensed as instructors themselves
(Wallis, 1977:119-20).

Rituals of Imitation

     This final category of manipulation rituals is designed
to give adherents a sense of control over their outer selves
and the world in which that outer self participates. In the
rituals of obedience, adherents learn to follow instructions,
not because obedience is a cherished quality, but because
learning to follow instructions minutely is one way to ensure
success in a technological, bureaucratic society. Imitation
rituals offer another kind of control. By learning expertly
to control the acts (or faces) that one is required to play,
one can control not only the outer personality but the outer
world. Once the 'act' is being directed by the internal self,
one can use the 'theatre' of the social environment to stage
plays with happy endings for the self. Consider the following
story, recounted by an Arica graduate:

          I began by asking him how going through Arica had
          changed his relationship to other people.
          A: Oh it's changed it a lot ... when I first met
          Aricans I thought they were kind of strange ...
          that they were overdramatic ... but that's because
          they were playing the theatre .... Aricans can
          always tell other Aricans ... but now I know how

to play the theatre. Like the other day I went into
the dry cleaners to get my dry cleaning and I saw it
hanging on a hook and nobody was around and I thought
... 'I could just reach over and take this' ... so I
just reached over and took it ... and the lady came
rushing out from the side and she was doing this
angry lady routine ... and in the past I would have
responded to this by getting defensive and saying I
wasn't stealing it and she would have probably said
I was stealing it but now I knew how to play the
theatre so I just went into my repentent polite young
man, and that neutralized her angry mother so she
could go back into the 'business woman'. You can help
people by neutralizing them.

- Arica interview

In the above anecdote, the Arica member experiences a
sense of power from being able to manipulate the 'act'. This
ability is largely seen as gained through a variety of role
playing techniques or rituals found in most "cult of man"
groups (SMC being the exception). Below is an example of
such a ritual drawn from Shakti and termed Daysnap.

The student draws a role or personality from a hat
and wears it for a specified amount of time. After
some practice, the game is extended outside the
centre (e.g. in a restaurant). A guide or group
accompanies the actor to prevent his over-
identification with the role. The goal is to be
able to perform any role efficiently, without
identification. (Palmer, 1976:84)

The notion that once the outer self is controlled, the
outer world is controlled, is repeated in several different
ritual contexts. The outer self and outer world seem to
"cause" events, but are in reality hollow, inanimate, pre-
programmed machines. The inner Self can allow these machines
to run, uncontrolled or can will itself to control them (be
"a cause"). The beginning steps are to regulate the actions
and responses of the personality self. Psychosynthesis has a
ritual called Turning the Switch in which adherents manipulate
those emotions attached to "personality" experiences by
turning them on and off at will. Once, however, the outer
self has been regulated, the outer world will fall into line,
in imitation. In one of the mose astounding rituals of
Scientology termed Waterloo Station, the entire outer world
is switched on and off in like fashion.

> The goal of Waterloo Station is not to make one thing
> vanish. That phenomenon is just the start. Auditors
> have been quitting when the preclear (student) made
> somebody's hat disappear. When the pc can make the
> whole universe wink on and off at his consideration
> to know or not know it, you're getting somewhere. So
> don't stop at the hat. (Wallis, 1977:115)

Similar uses of the will or power of the inner self to control and shape both external self and external world are explicitly linked to machines and machine technology. In a ritual called the Bio Cyb Theatre, Shakti members are connected to a wide variety of bio-cybernetic (feedback) equipment which in turn controls audiovisual equipment (lights, mood) and puts on a one-man sound and light show simply by controlling his nervous system (sweat, heat, blood, brain waves, etc.) (Palmer, 1976:82). The message of this ritual is clear. If the machine-self is controlled, so will the outer, artificial world of sound and light of which it is a part.

In conclusion, we have considered four kinds of manipulation rituals. These rituals deal with the control of the outer profane personality and may be seen to flow from the commitment to technology and the compromise with the rational secular world which characterizes "cult of man" groups. These groups accept and admit a world which is technologized, concerned with pragmatic efficiency and bureaucratic skills and which seems to run without the control of the individual human being. Success in such a world depends upon versatile and skillful performance of these programs, and yet, due to over-identification or emotional involvement with the "program," the individual may become confused and threatened, unable to perform a given "program" correctly or change programs. In short, she may fail to receive, encode, decode or correctly process the necessary information and may bungle the job. Purification rituals remove the "real Self" from such threats. Manipulation rituals teach careful processing techniques so that the threatening situations may be handled without error.

Finally, it is worth noting the advantages of this split view of the self. While the sectarian religious believer must shun worldly pursuits in order to dwell in the sacred, the "cult of man" member needs only to withdraw to her inner Self, leaving her body and outer personality to continue worldly activity without danger. This has the result of not only solving economic difficulties and of teaching adherents to survive successfully in a technological world and its bureaucracies, assuming and dropping "faces" at will, but also of giving them a sense of mystical power which can be used to shape and reshape the self and the world.

In Chapter X we will turn to a discussion of those specific rituals which serve to encourage and develop a sense of power, mastery and control, of which the rituals of manipulation discussed in this chapter are only an intimation.

CHAPTER X

INSIDE THE CONTROL ROOM:
RITUALS OF TRANSFORMATION

To date in this section, we have examined two distinct
but related kinds of rituals. In Chapter VIII we examined
rituals of purification. In these (negative) rituals the
sacred was carefully separated from the profane. This
involved a jolt which made adherents perceive a discrepancy
between outer personality and inner Self, followed by clear
demarcations of internal boundaries and the fortification of
the sacred Self by creation of an inner, psychic sanctuary
or lab. This involved a withdrawal of identification and/or
emotion from the outer personality.

In Chapter IX, we discussed those rituals dealing with
this outer personality, now empty of Self. We noted that it
was symbolized as a machine which could act to imprison the
Self if not properly controlled. Rituals were examined which
acted to control this machine, to get it to perform accurately
and efficiently at the command of the inner Self.

In the present chapter, we will examine a final set of
rituals which we call rituals of transformation. These deal
with the inner, sacred Self and its potential once separated
from the outer profane personality. These are clearly
'positive' rituals in Durkheim's terminology, not only because
they serve to allow for interaction between sacred Self and
profane world, but also because they serve to empower and
motivate adherents. Adherents may come to "cult of man"
groups because they need protection (purification) or to
master routine behavior in the world (manipulation) but it is
in the rituals of transformation that adherents find
experiences of power and ecstasy which are the reward for the
self-control demanded by purification and manipulation
rituals.

> While studying with intention in the privacy of my
> bedroom, I heard a noise in the adjoining den. I
> looked around to 'see' what it was, and behold, I
> looked right through the wall into the next room
> as though no wall was there. When your intention

> is very strong you can do what you intend to do.
> Wow! ... I love it -- like Superman.
>
>   - Scientology adherent from
>   (Wallis, 1976:121)

Wile the above experience, with its paranormal
implications, is one of the more extreme instances of the
powers which adherents feel accrue from transformational
rituals, the ecstatic response is similar in all such rituals.
Such ecstasy stems from the ability to transcend the normal
boundaries or limitations which most human beings experience.
This ability is achieved in, broadly, two categories of
transformational rituals: those which train adherents to
transcend the mortal limitations of their own bodies, and
those which allow them to enter into other substances. These
two categories of rituals express the same message about the
inner, sacred Self. If the outer personality is frozen and
restricted like a robot machine, the inner Self is a fluid
and unrestricted substance which may move and transform at
will.

Transcending the Limitations

All "cult of man" groups have rituals which, working
through the imagination or guided imagery, train the
adherents to leave their own bodies, to travel to places which
they could not physically go. In Scientology, this is called
'exteriorizing' and the goal of the ritual is to get the
adherent (called the 'preclear') to "give up the self-imposed
need to be in the body" (Wallis, 1976:114).

> Ask preclear to be three feet behind his head. If
> stable there, have him be in various pleasant
> places until any feeling of scarcity of viewpoints
> is resolved. Then have him be in several undesir-
> able places, then several pleasant places; then
> have him be in a slightly dangerous place, then in
> more dangerous places until he can sit in the centre
> of the Sun.
>
>   - Scientology Instruction Manual from
>   (Wallis, 1976:114)

Once outside the body, the person can travel where she
wills. In most of these groups there is a kind of astral
travel exercise where the members are guided on space
voyages. In est, this is called space travel (a ritual

exercise that takes several hours of intense imaginative visualization); in Scientology, it is called the Grand Tour. In Psychosynthesis and Silva Mind Control, guided imagery exercises involve the individual floating above the earth and looking down at the earth.

> The group leader told us to close our eyes and see where we were internally. Then we were to imagine we were outside the earth looking down at the earth, seeing where it was in the solar system, in the galaxy, in the universe. Then we were to move closer to the earth and see its colours and hear its sounds. Then we were to imagine that the earth were a person and see the qualities it had and see its characteristics and see where it was going and what it needed. And we should look into ourselves and our relationship with this person and what we had to give it. Then we were to come out slowly.
>
> - Psychosynthesis fieldnotes

It is worth noting, in passing, the subjective nature of these experiences. In a group like Scientology, adherents are told simply to locate themselves outside their bodies. In the Psychosynthesis exercise (one of those termed by the group 'guided imagery exercises') adherents are specifically instructed to 'imagine' that they are travelling in space. However, having performed the ritual, members discuss "what they experienced," meaning their private, personal imaginings and this experience is seen as real by all concerned. In other words, the images which the adherent received during the ritual are taken as messages from the Higher Self, as having a reality within the context of that Higher Self, and therefore as a guide to understanding the 'real' unlimited potential of that Higher Self. Being able to imagine being outside the earth is therefore seen as having the potential to be outside the earth, a potential which is in turn seen as a reality of the Higher Self. Most members of a group like Psychosynthesis perceive things like astral travel (outside of group context of ritual) as being real human possibilities, and so the line between subjective and objective reality is further blurred. As an Arica leader put it:

> In the province of the mind, what I believe to be true is true, or becomes true within certain limits to be found experientially and experimentally. These limits are further beliefs to be transcended. (Lilly, 1972:210)

Once outside the body, "cult of man" adherents find that not only can they travel through space, but through time. Arica members talk of visiting past lives and a Silva Mind Control graduate describes the following voyage experienced during one of the group's visualization rituals:

> On the last day of the course during a 'conditioning'
> I heard drums rolling like an army on the march. I
> was above the army and I could see the army. It had
> pipers and drummers and they were marching through
> the fields in off white uniforms, some on horses.
> In the fields in the distance guns were pointed ...
> then I saw some old barn full of Scotsmen, dancing
> and playing. I was annoyed and switched to a city
> with cheering crowds. I think it was the Crimean
> War.
>   - Silva Mind Control graduate

Having left the body and experienced travel through space and time, "cult of man" adherents are also ritually trained in entering matter other than their own bodies.

Re-entering Matter

A variety of rituals exist in "cult of man" groups to train adherents to enter plants, animals, metals and other people. The assumption behind this is that as the external, outer Self is machine-like and inanimate, its form is irrelevant. It has nothing to do with Self. The inner Self can therefore use it and discard it, assuming other forms as it chooses. To enter other forms is at once to experience the difference between outer and inner reality and to recognize the artificiality of the former.

On the second to last day of class, Silva Mind Control graduates are presented with four cylinders of metal: a copper cylinder, a steel cylinder, a brass cylinder and a lead cylinder. Holding these cubes to their foreheads, adherents are asked to project themselves into the metals. Up to this point, 'to project' has meant to imagine on the internal 'mental screen'. Now, however, it is used to mean 'enter into' as well as 'get a picture of'.

> We were told to enter into each cylinder in turn,
> gauging it for temperature, light, consistency and
> sound and smell. After the conditioning, people
> were asked what they had experienced. One woman
> said that the steel cube had appeared to her like
> a walk-in refrigerator. Another said that the

inside of the brass was like the inside of a tuba
and a third said that the inside of the steel was
a silver room with rainbow lights at the corners.
Someone remarked that the cubes seemed as big as
whole rooms. The woman who had experienced the
walk-in refrigerator was told that many people
experienced steel as the coldest metal. The
instructor said this was very useful ... now whenever this woman put her hand on a piece of metal
and thought of a walk-in refrigerator she could be
sure that the metal was steel.

- Silva Mind Control fieldnotes

Note, from the above sequence of events, that an
experience which might possibly have been interpreted as
'purely imaginative' by adherents is made real by the fact
that they are told that what the mind-in-alpha (or inner Self)
tells about the inside of the cylinder is real and this
information can be used in future to understand the world.

Silva Mind Control has similar exercises for entering
into and exploring plants and animals. As in the case above,
this involves a detailed guided tour of the various systems
within the plant and/or animal form. Scientology and est
also have adherents 'experience' such diverse objects as
lemons, strawberries, wood, a rock ("now find a rock; be
inside of it; be outside of it"). Psychosynthesis members
"become" blossoming rosebuds.

In a somewhat different but related manner, Psychosynthesis has a number of guided imagery rituals in which
members are asked to either pretend that they 'are' a certain
kind of animal, by assuming the outer gestures and expressions
of the animal or, conversely, to imagine that an animal exists
within them as in the following case:

Steve had never talked much up to this point in the
meetings, but today he began to complain about his
inner feelings of unexpressed intolerance. The
leader asked him to provide an image and Steve,
closing his eyes and concentrating, said that he
imaged a wolf, with his mouth open. He made the
corresponding face. The leader asked him to speak
as the wolf and to say why the mouth was open.
Steve said it was because he (the wolf) was hungry.
That he (the wolf) wanted people to watch out
because he would bite. That the wolf was intolerant
and didn't like people and if people could see the
angry wolf they wouldn't like him either. The

> leader said that animals often appeared to communicate
> things about the self.

- Psychosynthesis fieldnotes

It is important to note that in most transformational
rituals in "cult of man" groups, this sort of inside/out
confusion occurs. <u>The adherent enters into the plant, animal
or mineral by allowing the image of the plant, animal or
mineral to enter into him</u>. This is particularly vivid in the
case of those rituals dealing with the individual entering
another person.

The best example of this is undoubtedly drawn from the
healing ritual in Silva Mind Control. Leading up to this
ritual, members are given a booklet with the various human
organ systems illustrated in medical textbook forms. For the
ritual itself, the member projects the image of a sick person
on his or her "mental screen" (composing one wall of the
laboratory to which the adherent retires, mentally to perform
the healing ritual). Once the image of the sick person has
been projected on this internal screen, the adherent proceeds
to 'scan' the image, entering into the various systems
(digestive, nervous, cardiovascular) and travelling through
them to detect the parts which are malfunctioning.

While the healing ritual is performed on people whom
the adherent doesn't know, the skills attained by the adherent
in performing the ritual are used on people with whom the
adherent is familiar. For example, one SMC graduate who
confessed that he had always been very shy, explained how he
felt more confidence in his office and with a girl to whom he
had felt attracted. He explained that some of the other men
in his office thought her stuck-up, and at times unpleasant
but, after 'projecting' her on his own mental screen, he had
seen that she was very unhappy. He 'understood' her and was
no longer afraid of her.

This ability to get inside others is also expressed in
terms of telepathy:

> Yesterday I was walking down the main street. A woman
> ahead of me coming in the opposite direction was
> coughing badly. I put across to her -- telepathically
> -- 'are you OK?' When she got beside me she beamed
> and said "yes, that is a lot better now, thank you."

Well? The secret is in the OT (Operating Thetan)
Courses -- come and get it too.

- Scientology graduate
(Wallis, 1977:121)

At the end of the est training, adherents use new-found
telepathic and clairvoyant abilities to describe the
personality of persons they have never met by somehow "tuning
in" to their minds. We noted in Chapter VIII how, in the
Temple of the Sun ritual, the Psychosynthesis adherent meets
the other members of the group at the end of his internal
voyage to the centre of his own Self. Arica and est use
their internal 'psychic' spaces as places into which they may
bring other people, and may in turn 'get inside' them. Even
rituals like chanting are interpreted in Arica as a means of
merging with other people.

This time (in chanting) it was the whole group and I
was tuned into everybody. Everybody was me. I was
everybody ... like a baby in a womb. (Lilly, 1972:193)

It is interesting to note, in passing, the relationship
between these kinds of rituals and the belief in the "cast
of thousands" discussed in Chapter VI. This belief,
reflecting as it does a sense of internal fragmentation, may
be said to rest on the awareness of the adherent of a
multitude of different voices, roles and identities within,
which war for supremacy. One of the first steps in the
purification process, as noted in Chapter VIII, is to separate
the "real Self" from these shadow voices and identities.
Stripped of emotion and attachment, these become part of the
"other," that which is not Self. At the risk of reductionism,
one could argue that the vivid sense of relating in an inner
psychic place, to "other" people, may stem from a renewed
relationship with parts of the self, which, stripped of their
threat as possible identities, are seen as other people who
may be brought into the inner sanctuary to be examined,
analyzed, healed and dismissed without risk of contamination.
Such relationships clearly mark rituals as part of the
'positive' cult, governing the interaction between sacred and
profane:

This centre (the psychic, 'safe place') is the
equivalent of the training room, i.e. it is a safe

> place. The trainee can always go there in his
> imagination and work out situations with which he
> is having difficulty dealing. In addition, he can
> bring other people down into his center and talk
> to them without having fear of being reprimanded
> or that the information will be held against him.
> (Greene, 1976:92)

It is interesting to note that Silva Mind Control uses the term "projecting" to describe the experience of bringing the image of the unknown patient into the 'lab'. This term, borrowed from psychology, suggests that these patients are in fact parts of the self that the adherent visualizes. Psychosynthesis makes this point more explicit in their discussion of "reowning projections," i.e. recognizing that in reacting emotionally to others, one is really reacting to a projected part of the self. Silva Mind Control's pun on the word, to describe as well the projection of an image on a screen as in the case of film is significant in itself. What both groups then do is to deal with projections internally by objectification so that they become in the one case photographic, three-dimensional images, and in the other, characters in an internal cast.[4]

This process has a number of benefits. The "real self" is protected from threats of competing identities, external relationships with others are protected from the dangers of uncontrolled emotional interchanges, and the relationships between "real self" and the internal character-images not only have all the intensity of external interpersonal relations, but give rise to a sense of psychic power and control. While this explanation must be regarded as speculative, it does offer insight into one puzzling feature of the Silva Mind Control healing ritual. If in fact the internal projection carried on in the ritual gives adherents a covert opportunity to objectify, symbolize and 'heal' parts of the self, it is understandable that the ritual is overtly performed, not on friends but only on unknown strangers whose real bodily image cannot complicate or impinge on the process of psychological 'projection'.

This kind of psychological interpretation can, of course, be carried too far. What is important is that the internal "cast of thousands" can be seen to express a situation in which identity is confused, and also provide an arena for the development of the sense of psychic power, of being able to enter into and/or incorporate a vast number of individual personalities. This sense duplicates, on an interpersonal level, the rituals which train adherents to enter plants, minerals, animals and outer space.

In sum, then, transformational rituals in "cult of man" groups teach adherents to transcend the limitations of their external "mechanical" selves, to travel freely through time and space, to enter other forms at will.

What is even more interesting is that this sense of breaking through planes, or barriers, of transformative ability, is not unique to "cult of man" adherents. It has been attributed, cross-culturally and historically to shamans. This has been noted about some of these groups and attributed to western man's need for a spiritual path or "sadhana" (Ellwood, 1973) or the dawning of a new mythic consciousness (Larsen, 1977). The comparison, however, has been general, not detailed, and has failed to produce any kind of socio- logical analysis, having been derived, in general, from the "counterculture" theory of new religious movements. The parallel, however, between shamanic myth and "cult of man" group rituals is striking and deserves closer attention. In the remainder of this chapter we will compare the powers of "cult of man" adherents specifically to those of shamans, and discuss why such an association should occur in these groups.

The Genesis of the Shaman

A number of anthropologists have noted that a calling to a shamanic vocation is often heralded by the ability remarkably similar to that discussed in Chapter X to "break the planes." Among shamans this is interpreted as signifying the desire and ability to leave the body:

> What is the meaning of all these shamanic myths of
> ascent to Heaven and magical flight, or of the power
> to become invisible and incombustible? They all
> express a break with the universe of daily life.
> The break from plane to plane effected by flight or
> ascent similarly signifies an act of transcendence.
> Flight proves that one has transcended the human
> condition, has risen above it, by transmuting it
> through an excess of spirituality. (Eliade, 1958:
> 101)

For shamans, such powers of transcendence are, however, dependent on the successful completion of an initiation process, involving a symbolic death and rebirth marked by certain distinguishing characteristics. These include: (1) the summons, often marked by illness, trance or extreme disorientation, and heralded by the appearance of animals or snakes; (2) some kind of torture or dismemberment of the initiate (at times including cannibalism imagery); (3) the scraping away of the flesh until the body is reduced to the skeleton; (4) the substitution of viscera and the renewal of blood (including the incorporation of some 'sky' metal such as quartz or pearl into the body); (5) an encounter with spirits or demons who impart knowledge to the initiate, and (6) the aforementioned ascent into Heaven heralding the ability to transcend limitations (Eliade, 1958; Eliade, 1972; Larsen, 1977).

The rituals in "cult of man" movements do not, of course, duplicate these shamanic rituals exactly, but there is enough similarity between the two to be worth examining in greater detail. One may interpret the kind of tearing jolts described in Chapter VIII (purification rituals), the subsequent sense of inner fragmentation, the stripping away of the layers (as in the Psychosynthesis ritual of the Levels, or est's 'pain levels') to get at the real, the 'truth', the skeleton of the self as a kind of death by dismemberment, equivalent, on a psychological level, to steps (2) and (3) of shamanic initiation rites. The elaborate construction of the inner laboratory (and the careful, architectural mapping out of inner space, so that everything is 'clear') parallels the substitution of sky metal for viscera (step 4). Ellwood has noted, in groups like Scientology, what he considers the metaphorical version of replacing the internal viscera with quartz or crystal:

> The goal of occultists and initiates today is a new self of crystalline lucidity, permanence and luminosity. The groups they belong to believe it is possible for man to have states as different from his present condition as rock is from flesh, and much better able to withstand the viscissitudes of the world. (Ellwood, 1973:157)

By psychological analogy, therefore, one may say that
"cult of man" groups act out the death and rebirth of the
primitive shaman: stripping away of old self and building up
a new "clear" powerful being.

However, the similarity is not solely analogous and
extends to the language used by members to describe their
experience. "Cult of man" groups do use actual images of
animal heralds, dismemberment, stripping of the physical self
and incorporation of new viscera uncannily similar to those
used in shamanic myth. For example, Psychosynthesis uses a
great deal of animal imagery to herald the awakening of higher
powers:

> For me, the biggest thing was the Will ... it changed
> my whole life. I wasn't in touch with my Will ... I
> thought the power was with other people ... I didn't
> realize I could do whatever I chose to do. As I
> began to get in touch with Will, it came out in all
> sorts of ways. I began to get all kinds of snake
> images, but I was afraid of snakes, I didn't know
> what they meant. Then I went on a boat trip and
> one morning we were anchored near shore and I got
> up early in the morning and went for a swim. I
> was standing on the shore, naked, feeling wonderful,
> washing my hair when I saw this little black head
> bobbing through the water. It was a snake. I was
> terrified and then I looked in the water to the
> right and there was curled up another red snake
> and I looked and there was a yellow snake on the
> other side. About this time crazy things started
> to happen. A wooden motor boat with no windows
> went by and then I was divebombed by this little
> plane, which swooped down on me and landed on the
> island. I said to myself I can do one of two
> things ... I can faint, or I can swim to my boat
> ... so I plunged in and swam through the snakes.
> I can tell you that was the hardest thing I
> have ever done ... it was a powerful experience ...
> and then I remembered that about three weeks before
> that I had got an image ... in an exercise (Psycho-
> synthesis) about what I needed in order to become
> what I wanted. I got this image of three snakes,
> the one in the middle was straight up and down and
> the ones on the sides curled around it until it
> made the symbol of healing. Boy, your Higher Self
> has ways of telling you and if you don't listen
> things get arranged so you can't ignore it.
>
> - Psychosynthesis member

This anecdote has a distinct "mythic" quality, not only in
the image of the three snakes, but in the image of the diving
plane, and the strange boat without windows. The adherent saw

in the experience a powerful message which had been given to
her before in the form of an image visualized in a Psychosynthesis exercise. The goal of the exercise had been self-
development, and the adherent had misunderstood and ignored
the image as it seemed obscure. Events then occurred which
forced her not only to understand the message but to act on
it: to use her inner power or her Will. In like manner, the
primitive shaman may aspire to become a "Man of Power" and
may practice for the vocation, but when the calling comes,
"it comes suddenly and totally other than one's expectations":

> The vision may come in the form of a great owl which
> brutally knocks one bleeding into the snow, leaving
> no doubt that the spirit is totally other than one-
> self; or a fierce walrus, a wolverine or a snake.
> And sometimes the call may come in the form of an
> omen, a series of events, the import of which a
> mythically unattuned mind might pass right by.
> (Larsen, 1977:79)

For shamans, the stage following the summons or call is
the death by torture and dismemberment. This stage, too can
be found represented in graphic terms in some "cult of man"
groups. For instance, Shakti uses numerous images of
cannibalism (which are also associated in shamanic myth with
the early stages of torture and dismemberment) talking of
eating and being eaten. Shakti leader, E. J. Gold, published
a colouring book entitled "A Child's Guide to
Transubstantiation" and including the following sentiments,
among others:

> I have a pet chicken named Harry when he dies
> I am going to eat him, yum.
> When you are eaten by someone then you are
> suddenly inside everybody and you can see every-
> where at once. (Palmer, 1976:56)

A Shakti member also produced the following anecdote to
express the experience of 'ego' destruction:

> A sailor on a transatlantic journey was suffering
> from a case of the clap. He went to a doctor at the
> next port who said, "There's nothing I can do. It
> will have to be cut off." He waited two weeks to con-
> sult another doctor at the next port who gave the same
> advice. Refusing to accept it, he waited until he was
> home in acute pain, the member swollen and turning all
> colours of the rainbow. He found the top specialist
> in V. D. in the city and said, "Please doctor, don't

tell me to cut it off!" The doctor took one look and replied, "You don't have to cut it off. In another couple of days it will fall off by itself." (Palmer, 1976:57)

This is dismemberment with a vengeance. The moral of the story is that the outer self or ego must be shed: if you don't cut it off it will fall off by itself.

The language used in this story is shamanic in tone and in intent. It reveals the shamanic sense of vocation: unless the outer self is discarded it will cause tremendous pain and anguish.

The "Child's Guide to Transubstantiation," on the other hand, illustrates how to eat and be eaten is linked to the powers subsequently attained by shamans, of being able to be in all things and people. This casts a new light on the Psychosynthesis ritual of "acting out in the centre" (Chapter VIII) and the use of cannibalistic terms by members themselves when discussing the ritual. The person who "acted out" did so in order to 'grow', to develop her own inner potential (or psychic powers). In order to realize that potential, however (which included the ability to incorporate and enter into others in a psychic sense), she needed to ritually climb into 'the pot' and 'feed' the group with her emotions and psychic self. Then she was "inside everybody" and could "see everything at once."

In addition to their metaphoric dismemberment of parts of the psychic self, therefore, "cult of man" adherents actually use images of physical dismemberment and cannibalism. Similarly, while Psychosynthesis may talk of stripping away the psychic layers, in the Silva Mind Control healing ritual and in the exercises leading up to it, students imaginatively strip away physical skin, muscle and nervous tissue to reveal the human skeleton (of their own and others' bodies) and sort through the viscera, replacing any parts that are malfunctioning. Once again, this ritual refers quite graphically to the physical self in terms similar to the shamanic myth.

The shamanic image of replacing the internal viscera with crystal or quartz is echoed not only in the elaborate internal architecture constructed by Aricans (whose 'psychic space' is a glass pyramid), but also in the Silva Mind Control ritual of

projecting metals. Bearing in mind the description of the
steel cylinder as "a silver room with rainbow lights at the
corners," consider the following qualities of the mythical
shamanic crystals:

> The initiatory operations proper always include the
> renewal of the organs and viscera, the cleaning of
> the bones, and the insertion of magical substances
> -- quartz, crystals or pearl shell, or "spirit
> snakes." Quartz is connected with the "sky world
> and with the rainbow"; pearl is similarly "connected
> with the rainbow serpent" that is, in sum, the sky.
> The sky symbolism goes along with the ecstatic
> ascents to Heaven. (Eliade, 1958:99)

The silver and rainbow quality of the metal, as well as
its hardness and its connection with the powers of transformation, suggest that the SMC ritual parallels the
replacement of the viscera in shamanic initiation.

Finally, the "cult of man" trainees receive spirit
helpers to instruct them in their new powers. As noted
earlier, Silva Mind Control graduates receive two 'spirit
guides' to help them solve problems in the lab. For Arica,
these guides have names: they are the 'angels' Thelmo and
Ulmo. In Psychosynthesis, the voice of the Higher Self speaks
in the image of a wise old man or woman, or from the center of
the sun. This voice can be relied upon as a guide and help-
mate and will answer any question.

With the help of these guides the "cult of man" adherent
"ascends into the Heavens," as characteristic of the final
stage of shamanic initiation in the rituals of leaving the
body and astral travel, discussed at the beginning of this
chapter.

In sum, "cult of man" members experience many of the
features of shamanic initiation, in the same terms as those
used in the shamanic myth. They experience 'calling' often in
the form of an animal-herald, dismemberment, stripping to the
bone and replacement of viscera both by analogy (in terms of
the corresponding psychological imagery) and in terms of the
symbolism of physical death and rebirth used by shamans. The
"cult of man" member receives aid while going through this
process, in the form of helping spirits, and she attains
transformative powers similar to those received by shamans.

This similarity between "cult of man" groups and shamans is all the more interesting as it appears unconscious on the part of the "cult of man" groups. The leaders and members of these movements do not self-consciously identify themselves as Shamans, as, for example, do contemporary witches and Satanists. They do not see themselves as workers of magic, so much as 'self-realized' human beings.

If such imagery is not self-consciously employed, there remains to attempt some explanation about why it has been so systematically adopted by "cult of man" groups. What is it about shamanic myth and symbol that is so appealing to these groups, or, conversely, what aspect of group experience does the imagery express?

"The shaman is a man who can die and return to life many times," notes Eliade (1958). The unifying feature in all the mythic powers of the shaman and of "cult of man" members is the ability to cross boundaries: those of life and death, time and space, and physical bodies, animate and inanimate. If we analyze this in social-structural terms, as Douglas would have us do, it suggests that the shaman is someone able not only to move in and out of social categories (through social boundaries) at will, but also to exist in the inter-stices without danger. He may, in other words, be 'faceless' without danger, and assume any 'face' he chooses at will.

It is interesting in this context, to note what Douglas has to say about shamans (Douglas, 1966:114-136). She notes that in any society there are two kinds of power. The first is the power linked to the social structure and attached to those in positions of legitimate authority which she terms the power of 'form'. The second is power existing in the margins, outside of the lines which distinguish and demarcate social order. This is the power of "formlessness," disorder and chaos, and represents danger to the order. This is one of the reasons, as we noted in Chapter VIII, that people in transitional states are thought of as dangerous and endangered; they dwell in the "formless" regions between social categories or social states.

For Douglas, several classes of people other than initiates, have access to the power of formlessness. Among them are witches, sick men and shamans. She distinguishes

between witches and shamans because witchcraft is attributed
to those who exist perpetually in the margins, playing
ambiguous and interstitial social roles. Shamans, however,
have access both to "formlessness" and its power and to
legitimate authority. For Douglas, the relationship between
the sick man and the shaman is that both enter into
"disordered regions of the mind" which are symbolic of the
"disordered regions of society." Unlike the sick man,
however, the shaman returns from those regions to occupy a
position of honour and power within the social order.

> The man who comes back from these inaccessible regions
> (of the mind or of society) brings with him a power
> unavailable to those who have stayed in the control of
> themselves and of society. (Douglas, 1966:115)

What's more, Douglas suggests that shamanism and sorcery
abound in those societies which have a weakened sense of
order where the difference between legitimate and illegitimate
authority isn't clear, and where, therefore, legitimate
authority is somewhat "up for grabs." This is because sorcery
is not an innate quality necessarily, but something that can
be acquired through training and is therefore potentially
available to everyone. Of course, in such a society, the
order is weak and easily penetrated (Douglas, 1966:130).

If we return to our "cult of man" data with Douglas'
theories in mind, we have a potential explanation for the
appeal of shamanic imagery. In Chapter VII, we identified
the "cult of man" member as someone who felt 'faceless',
permanently endangered, between categories, moving from one
insubstantial 'face' to another. This was attributed to the
necessity of changing social categories and/or 'form'
frequently. The "cult of man" adherent was defined as
continually required to move from 'form' to 'formlessness' to
new 'form', from 'face' to 'facelessness' to new 'face', with
resulting sense of danger and contamination. Fear results
from the transition, from the loss of 'form' and ensuing
identity crisis on the one hand, to the resumption of form and
the fear of failure on the other. In Chapter IX we noted how
manipulation rituals help to reduce the latter fear, giving
adherents a sense of access to the power of 'form'. Transformational rituals, on the other hand, reduce the former

fear, giving adherents a sense of access to the power of 'formlessness'.

In this context, it is easier to understand the excitement which adherents find in transformational rituals. It is the excitement of being able to ride the liquid wave of reality, becoming a skilled amphibian. Adherents may still experience the world and people in it as in continual transition, but now, instead of drowning and becoming lost in this dangerous flux, the transformational rituals provide (at least by suggestion) mastery of this condition, similar to the shaman's mastery. One still 'dies and is born again' continually to different identities but one is "at cause" in choosing the identity. In a magical transformation, one can become what and whom one pleases (a mystical seventies version of the old North American utilitarian individualism). This knowledge is coupled with a sense of triumph for "cult of man" adherents; they are in control, they have seized the reins. They are, indeed, "empowered."

The feeling of seizing power is not strictly limited to the magical and the psychic. Mastery of 'formlessness' seems to lead to increased mastery of 'form', generalizing to everyday life and the social order to which the adherents belong. As noted in this chapter, getting inside another person can signify to the "cult of man" adherent anything from psychic healing at a distance to "casing out" the pretty girl in the office; transcending bodily limitations can range from astral travel to checking out the noise in the next room by looking through the wall instead of around it. In addition, there is some indication that the "cult of man" adherents do not distinguish between legitimate and illegitimate power but see sorcery in the most prosaic of occupations and "legitimate" authority as up for grabs:

> The energy itself is completely value free. It's like the Force in Star Wars ... you can use it for negative and positive reasons. I'm very judgemental ... I feel that people shouldn't use it for material gain, but who says it's evil? People in the stock market use it for intuition ... to control the flow of money and how to use it. They use it to get what they want.
>
> - Psychosynthesis member

> The politicians don't have the power ... they are run
> by multinational corporations ... they're just playing
> a game. I wouldn't distinguish between politicians
> and mafia, or police and criminals. They're all play-
> ing the same game ... whether you're a cop or a
> criminal depends largely on which side of the track
> you are brought up on ... it's just power.
>
> - Arica member

It is impossible without more systematic interview data
to determine how widespread in "cult of man" groups (and
elsewhere) is the kind of cynicism expressed in the above two
quotes. If in fact they are representative, they indicate,
again, that the "cult of man" adherents' experience of social
reality is one of confusion of form and formlessness:
confused social order and power up for grabs. It is such a
situation, precisely, which Douglas suggests the shamanic
myth reflects.

Not to push the comparison too far, it seems necessary
at this point to mention the differences between shamans and
"cult of man" adherents. Shamans are isolated individuals
whereas the "cult of man" is a group. The shaman is
recognized by the wider society as holding a valuable
occupational role merely by being a shaman, whereas most "cult
of man" adherents hold roles unrelated to their "shamanic"
abilities. Finally, the shaman uses his powers on behalf of
the community. He leaves his body to bring gifts to the gods
from the community, communicates with a dead soul for the
community, brings back the soul of a sick man who has
wandered (Eliade, 1958). The "cult of man" adherent performs
these operations on his outer self on behalf of his Inner
Self. For these groups the shamanic imagery seems to have
less to do with becoming "men of power," manipulating their
outer environment as the primitive shaman did, and more to do
with the fact that such imagery is highly expressive of the
experience of continual flux, moving from 'form' to 'formlessness'. "Cult of man" adherents group together because
this is a common experience for them, not an idiosyncratic
one as in the case of the primitive shaman.

In conclusion, it would be reasonable to suggest that the
rituals of transformation, which we have discussed in this
chapter, represent the positive or empowering aspects of a
social experience of 'facelessness' discussed in Chapter VII.

If one exists in a world where lines are vague and inadequate, one experiences terror and contamination; protection and control are necessary. One may also, however, become a master of flux, or transformation, of the ephemeral image. In short, one may become like a shaman who dies and is reborn, whose insides are crystal clear but who possesses multiple faces. Besides reducing fear (by providing a chameleon-like protective covering) and inducing ecstasy, becoming such a master also has the power to produce a much needed sense of continuity and identity. For, as Eliade has pointed out, part and parcel of the shaman's transformational ability is the ability to "remember" various forms, experiences and existences.

> He has succeeded in integrating into consciousness a
> considerable number of experiences that for the pro-
> fane world are reserved for dreams, madness and post-
> mortem states. (Eliade, 1958:102)

We may now understand the emphasis on memory in "cult of man" groups: Shakti's insistence that the individual learn to "eliminate the blackout between lives," est's emphasis on digging down through the pain levels to remember forgotten segments of this life, Silva Mind Control's elaborate rituals for developing and maintaining memory. Rituals of transformation (coupled as they are with the emphasis on memory) allow the individual to express the fragmentation of self, the sense of boundlessness while simultaneously typing together these fragments in a Higher Self, who sees and remembers. Thus held together, the individual can continue to operate in a fragmented, complex and diverse world.

CHAPTER XI

CONCLUSION: THE QUESTION OF ETHICS

In this dissertation, we have made use of Emile Durkheim's hypotheses about religion in modern society to explore and analyze new religious movements from a fresh perspective. Combining Durkheim's view of the religion of the past and of the future and bringing this to bear on the present has hopefully produced a number of insights into the beliefs, organization and ritual of the contemporary groups we labelled "cult of man" groups.

First and foremost, what this dissertation has tried to indicate is that groups holding the human individual sacred are present in contemporary society (in the form of 'transpersonal trainings') and that Durkheim's theories of religion, far from being inapplicable to modern religion, are valuable in understanding and documenting the unique character of these movements.

In Chapters V and VI we noted that, true to Durkheim's basic postulate about religion, the elements of belief in "cult of man" groups reflect elements of the social organization of those groups. Combined, they present a picture of religious life distinct from contemporary groups which locate the sacred outside the individual, as well as from the harmonial groups of the early 1900's which, while sharing the basic 'cult' organization of the "cult of man," are less extreme in these features. In short, the particular notion of the sacred held by "cult of man" groups, that it is the ideal human individual that is sacred, does seem related to the diversity and complexity of modern life, as Durkheim suggested it would be.

In Chapter VII, we examined this connection more closely. Using Douglas' notion of pollution and threats to boundaries to analyze the fears of interpersonal contamination present in these groups, it was suggested that these fears reflect a sense of 'facelessness' which in turn reflects the personal and social flux individual adherents of "cult of man" groups experience in their urban, bureaucratic environment. It was

167

also indicated that, due to their particular occupations and lifestyles, "cult of man" adherents are more likely than normal to be exposed to the instabilities and confusions of modern life.

In the ensuing section on ritual, we took a closer look at the details of "cult of man" trainings, again using Durkheim's notion that ritual acts overtly to regulate relations between the sacred and the profane and covertly to regulate relations between the individual and society. It was noted that rituals in the "cult of man" were divided into two categories as in primitive religion: negative (discouraging and controlling relations) and positive (encouraging and shaping relations). It was in the ritual context that the most unique features of the "cult of man" groups became apparent. It appeared that as the sacred was located within the individual, rituals became privatistic, concerned with regulating of the relationship of outer and inner self. In short, ritual continued to perform the same function that Durkheim suggested it had in the past, but in the context of a single individual.

In addition, however, the rituals in the "cult of man" reinforce the picture of modern society drawn in the chapter on beliefs. The rituals are orientated to regulating relations in a world in which both individual and society are continually in a state of flux. The negative rituals, the aim of which in primitive society is the protection of the sacred, take the form of purification rituals in "cult of man" groups, demanding great emotional control and interactional precision in interpersonal relationships. The positive rituals, the aim of which is the shaping of the interaction between sacred and profane, take the form of transformational rituals in "cult of man" groups, giving the adherents a sense of mastery of the flux and of intimate connection to all other people on an inner, psychic level.

In summary, then, the beliefs of groups like Psycho-synthesis, est and Silva Mind Control concerning the sacred, and the relationship of these beliefs to the group organiza-tion, rituals and the larger social system correspond to the individual elements of the "cult of man" as Durkheim described it. The individual human being (idealized) is held sacred,

and this belief does seem to be expressive of the complexity
and diversity of modern life, conducive to making people feel
they have "nothing in common." Adherents do feel that what
they have in common is their sacred humanity, and join
together to be empowered and motivated by this inner union.
In addition, such groups are heavily reliant on social science
and science to explain society to them; their 'representation'
of society is largely expressive.

Nevertheless, we should not overlook the fact that in at
least one regard -- respect for the rights of others --
contemporary "cult of man" groups diverge from Durkheim's
ideal. When Durkheim devised his theory about the future of
religion, he was concerned centrally with the problem of
maintaining order and social solidarity in a society in which
individualism would become increasingly pronounced due to
specialization and diversity in the social system. He felt
that commitment and motivation would be available in such a
society only through a religion of the individual. Such a
religion would create a space around the individual similar to
the space created around all sacred objects. Infringement on
the individual's rights or person would be received by the
others in that society with the kind of passionate indignation
traditionally associated with a profanation of the sacred.

This kind of concern with the rights of others is con-
spicuously absent in "cult of man" groups. It is not that
they preach disregard or lack of concern for others. In fact,
many are concerned with helping others to reach or realize
their inner potential. But due to the split between outer and
inner self, adherents feel that outer behavior has little to
do with the sacred, inner self. When asked, for example, what
they would do if witness to a physical or emotional attack of
one individual on another, a typical response was:

> I would ask the abusing person if they wanted feedback.
> If they said no, I wouldn't interfere. The person
> isn't ready, doesn't want help ... so I'd wait. If the
> violence was physical I wouldn't interfere unless I
> felt centered enough at that point ... my goal would
> not be to stop it ... but I'd ask the person 'do you
> want to keep doing this'?
>
> - Psychosynthesis interview

In short, it appears that the space separating the holy
which Durkheim envisioned as <u>around</u> each individual for contemporary "cult of man" adherents exists <u>within</u> each
individual, separating inner from outer self. It is the inner
Self which is revered, and this inner Self finds little or no
expression in outer behavior. In addition, the sacred inner
Self exists within <u>all</u> individuals, abuser and the abused
alike, and is worth equal respect wherever it is found. In
the above quote, it is the <u>abuser</u> who concerns the speaker.
The abuser seems to be out of control and hence his inner Self
is in danger. The abused, presumably, may still be in
control, i.e. unattached or disidentified with the outer
events, and is so not a source of worry. Outer behavior is
only a symptom of the inner state ... it is not in itself a
source of concern. After all, for "cult of man" adherents,
abuser and abused are in fact indistinguishable, both parts of
the outer artificial reality.

Does such an anti-interventionist policy belie a
narcissistic preoccupation with self? Not necessarily. For
there is some evidence in all these groups of a kind of
service ethic. "Cult of man" adherents may not intervene on
the behalf of the outer personality, but they do seem to
exhibit some concern with intervention on behalf of the inner,
sacred nature. This is done in two ways: by exemplary
behavior which makes manifest the high degree of inner
spiritual development and by helping those who request it to
learn to develop their own inner potential.

In the first instance are cases like the highly
publicized est anti-hunger campaign and the image of the ideal
human being held up for Psychosynthesis members to admire.

> The sign of the ideal person in psychosynthesis terms
> is the person engaged in active service ... he's not
> necessarily famous, but humanitarian. PS suggests
> people like Schweitzer and Gandhi .... This kind of
> person has balanced fully their emotions; mind and
> body are balanced. Once balance is achieved in the
> personality, then the Higher Self can enter.
>
> - Psychosynthesis member

Here, again, the actions in the world appear to be valued
largely in terms of what they symbolize about the state of
development of the Higher Self, but the action (no matter why

motivated) is 'exemplary' in its selfless service to others.
By transforming the self, the "cult of man" adherent believes
one can transform the world.

How many adherents actually engage in such 'exemplary'
service and to what extent is questionable and would provide
a fruitful area for further research. Also questionable is
the "cult of man" adherents' desire to help others to realize
this potential. It would seem most adherents who become
deeply involved in the trainings eventually become trainers
themselves, but concrete data on this issue is also required.

What remains clear, however, is that while this attitude
to their fellow humans' worldly rights almost certainly
represents a departure from Durkheim's image of his "cult of
man," these groups do seem to encourage a commitment to that
larger social system and so help to maintain order. The
identification of the outer self as a machine is compatible
with the mechanical, controlled world of the modern
bureaucracy. The emphasis on 'tuning up' this machine, on
improving its efficient and rational operation, increasing
its precision and decreasing its affect would all appear to
create a kind of elective affinity between "cult of man"
groups and the highly rationalized order of a bureaucratic,
technological society. While members may not be 'attached'
to this outer system any more than they are, ideally
'attached' to their outer personalities, they, nevertheless,
confirm it by their action and their philosophy.

In the last analysis, it is difficult to dismiss these
groups as either disintegrative or narcissistic. Whether, on
the other hand, they offer solutions to any of our existing
social problems, is questionable and awaits the test of time
and further research.

In sum, this dissertation has tried to demonstrate that
in that aspect which Durkheim saw as most central to modern
religion, its expressive potential, the "cult of man" groups
succeed brilliantly. In the beliefs and rituals of these
groups, we have seen an acute sensitivity to personal and
cultural flux, to the complexity and diversity of the modern
society. In their shamanic attitude to this flux, the feeling
that one may capitalize on it, as opposed to escaping it or
trying to diminish it, these individuals are expressing their

potential not only as individuals but as virtuosi members of
a modern social system characterized by rapid and continual
change. In such expression we may find as much cause for
optimism as for pessimism. As Bellah has put it so well:

> It is the chief characteristic of the more recent
> modern phase that culture and personality themselves
> have to be viewed as endlessly revisable. This has
> been characterized as a collapse of meaning and a
> failure of moral standards. It remains to be seen
> whether the freedom modern society implies at the
> cultural and personal as well as the social level
> can be stably institutionalized in large-scale
> societies. Yet the very situation which has been
> characterized as one of collapse of meaning can
> also, and I would argue more fruitfully, be viewed
> as one offering unprecedented opportunities for
> creative innovation in every sphere of human action.
> (Bellah, 1970:44)

The members of the groups themselves claim that the
transformation of society depends upon the transformation of
the individual in it. On closer examination of groups which
this dissertation has tried to provide, this catch phrase
may be interpreted somewhat less simplistically. If the
transformation of the individual implies creating personal
fluidity, an ability to handle change and diversity, a
versatility and adaptability, then the survival of those same
qualities in modern, industrial society may well depend on a
vision of human potential similar to that of the "cult of
man."

[1] The author is particularly indebted to Susan Palmer (Shakti), Paul Schwartz and Elizabeth Sandul (CCR). However, over the years, there has been much discussion and exchange of ideas among all team members. The author is therefore also indebted for these discussions to Scott Davidson, Bill Wheeler, Hugh Shankland, Joan Perry, Karina Rosenberg, Charlie Small, Daryl Leavitt, Katherine McMorrow, Rich Frankl, Judith Castle and Professors Bird and Reimer.

[2] The Catholic Charismatic Renewal Movement (CCR) originated in the U.S. in 1969; as a result, it is thought, of the 'looser' atmosphere created by Vatican II and a development of the Cursillo movement in the U.S. Basically a pentacostal revival, it seems at times quite distinct from traditional Catholicism. It is, nevertheless, largely housed in parish halls and is often led (particularly in Quebec) by Catholic priests and nuns. Studies have also shown that the majority of those recruited to the movement were of Catholic faith before joining and their faith, if anything, is strengthened by participation in the movement. Hence a compromise is being worked out in most cases, between traditional Catholicism and Pentacostalism.

CCR adherents place special emphasis on the Holy Spirit and his 'gifts'. These include glossolalia or speaking in tongues, prophecy, wisdom, healing (mental and physical) teaching and several others.

The groups in Montreal represented in this dissertation are three: a small, English speaking group, a large English speaking group, and a small French speaking group. All three were led by Catholic priests.

[3] It is supported ideologically, however. While the turn-of-the-century cults do not reject the world as the sects do, they are, nevertheless, at great pains, according to Mann, to separate their approach to Christianity from traditional or dogmatic forms, to the extent that they are actively hostile to church and sect. Contemporary "cult of man" groups make no such distinction and so make it even easier for members to simultaneously hold a variety of loyalties.

[4] This would appear to be an excellent example of what Durkheim thought of as faith anticipating science and forcing early closure. The concept of "projection" is used in Psychosynthesis in its correct psychological manner. It is then, however, reified and projections become distinct personalities with names (such as "The Analyst," "The Bystander") who are manipulated imaginatively to make them speak, interact and walk in and out of doors.

REFERENCES

Adler, N. 1975. "Ritual, Release and Orientation." In
    Religious Movements in Contemporary America. I. Zaretsky
    and M. Leone (eds.). Princeton, N. J.: Princeton
    University Press: 283-297.

Anthony, D. and R. Robbins. 1975. "The Meyer Baba Movement."
    In Religious MOvements in Contemporary America.
    I. Zaretsky and M. Leone (eds.). Princeton, N. J.:
    Princeton University Press: 479-511.

    1978. "A Typology of Non-Traditional Religious Movements
    in America." Unpublished manuscript.

Bach, K. W. 1973. Beyond Words. Baltimore, Maryland:
    Penguin Books.

Bellah, R. 1970. Beyond Relief. New York: Harper and Row.

Berger, P. 1970. "Between System and Horde." In Movement
    and Revolution. P. Berger and R. Neuhaus (eds.). New
    York: Doubleday.

    1973. The Homeless Mind. New York: Vintage Books.

Bird, F. 1978. "Charisma and Ritual in New Religious
    Movements." In Understanding the New Religions. Edited
    by J. Needleman and George Baker. New York: Seabury
    Press.

Brown, Peter. 1975. Augustine of Hippo. Berkeley,
    California: University of California Press.

Bry, A. 1976. 60 Hours That Transform Your Life: Est. New
    York: Harper and Row.

Douglas, M. 1966. Purity and Danger. London: Routledge
    and Kegan.

    1978. Natural Symbols. New York: Penguin Books.

Durkheim, Emile. 1897. "Labriola, Antonia. Essais sur la
    conception materialiste de l'histoire," RP XLIV:
    645-51 (as trans. in S. Lukes, 1975, Emile Durkheim.
    London: Penguin Books: 231).

    1899. "Da la definition des phénomènes religieux."
    L'Année sociologique, vol. 11: 1-28.

    1919. "Contribution to F. Abauzit et al. Le sentiment
    religieux a l'heure actuelle." Paris: Vrin (as
    quoted in S. Lukes, 1975, Emile Durkheim: His
    Life and Work. Great Britain: Peregrine Press:
    519).

175

1951. (1897). Suicide: A Study in Sociology.
Translated by J. A. Spaulding and G. Simpson.
Glencoe, Ill.: Free Press of Glencoe.

1953. (1924). "Sociology and Philosophy." Translation
of 1924 by J. A. Spaulding and G. Simpson.
Glencoe, Ill.: Free Press of Glencoe.

1961. (1913). Elementary Forms of the Religious Life.
New York: Collier Books.

1969. (1898). "Individualism and the Intellectuals."
Translation of 1898 article by S. and J. Lukes
with note, in Political Studies, XVII: 14-30.

Eister, A. 1975. "Cultural Crisis and New Religious Move-
ments." In Religious Movements in Contemporary America.
I. Zaretsky and M. Leone (eds.). Princeton, N. J.:
Princeton University Press: 612-27.

Eliade, Mircea. 1958. Rites and Symbols of Initiation. New
York: Harper Torchbooks.

1968. The Sacred and the Profane. New York: Harper
and Row.

1972. Shamanism: Archaic Techniques of Ecstasy.
Princeton, N. J.: Princeton University Press.
Bollingen Series.

Ellwood, R. S. 1973. Religious and Spiritual Groups in
Modern America. New Jersey: Prentice-Hall Inc.

Fenn, R. 1972. "A New Sociology of Religion." In JSSR,
vol. 11, No. 1, March: 16-32.

Gaustad, E. S. 1974. A Religious History of America. New
York: Harper and Row.

Gerlach and Hines. 1970. People, Power and Change. New
York: Bobbs-Merrill.

Gerth, H. H. and C. Wright Mills (eds.). 1958. From Max
Weber. New York: Oxford University Press.

Glock, C. and R. Bellah. 1976. The New Religious Consciousness. Berkeley, California: University of California
Press.

Goffman, E. 1961. Asylums. New York: Anchor Books.

Goffman, E. 1963. Behavior in Public Places. New York:
The Free Press.

1967. Interaction Ritual. New York: Doubleday.

Gold, E. J. 1973. The Shakti Handbook, P. O. Box 1556,
Crestline, California. Core Group Publication.

Greene, W. 1976. est 4 days to Make Your Life Work.
Markham, Ontario: Pocket Books.

Harrison, M. I. 1974. "Sources of Recruitment to Catholic
Pentacostal Movement." Journal for the Scientific Study
of Religion, 13: 49-64.

Ichazo, Oscar. 1976. The Human Process for Enlightenment
and Freedom. New York: Arica Institute.

Johnson, Benton. 1963. "Church and Sect." American
Sociological Review, 28, No. 4 (August 1963): 539-49.

Johnson, G. 1976. "The Hare Krishna in San Francisco." In
C. Glock and R. Bellah, The New Religious Consciousness.
Berkeley, California: University of California Press:
31-51.

Judah, J. Stillson. 1967. The History and Philosophy of
Metaphysical Movements in America. Philadelphia:
Westminster Press.

Keene, R. C. 1974. "Formal Organization and Charisma in a
Catholic Pentacostal Community." Unpublished Ph.D.
dissertation, University of Michigan.

Larsen, Stephen. 1977. The Shaman's Doorway: Opening the
Mythic Imagination to Contemporary Consciousness.
New York: Harper Colophon Books.

Lasch, C. 1975. "The Emotions of Family Life." New York
Review of Books, vol. 22, 19 (November): 37-42.

Lifton, R. J. 1969. "Protean Man." In Religious Situation.
Donald R. Cutler (ed.). Boston: Beacon Press, Inc.:
812-28.

Lilly, John. 1972. The Eye of the Cyclone. New York:
Bantam Books.

Lofland, J. 1966. Doomsday Cult. Englewood Cliffs, New
Jersey: Prentice-Hall.

Luckmann, T. and Peter Berger. 1964. "Social Mobility and
Personal Identity." European Journal of Sociology, 5:
331-43.

Lukes, S. 1975. Emile Durkheim: His Life and Work. Great
Britain: Peregrine Books.

Malko, G. 1971. Scientology, The Now Religion. New York:
Delacarte Press.

Mann, W. E. 1972. Sect, Cult and Church in Alberta.
Toronto: University of Toronto Press.

Marin, P. 1975. "The New Narcissism." Harper's Magazine
(October): 46-56.

Marty, Martin. 1970. "The Occult Establishment." Social
    Research 37(2): 212-230.

McGuire, M. 1975. "Toward a Sociological Interpretation of
    CCR." Review of Religious Research: 94-104.

Needlemann, J. 1970. The New Religions. New York:
    Doubleday & Co.

Nelson, G. K. 1969. Spiritualism and Society. London:
    Routledge & Kegan Paul.

Ornstein, R. 1975. A Self-Report Survey: Preliminary Study
    of Participants in Erhard Seminars Training. New York:
    est Foundation.

Orr, J. B. and F. Patrick Nicholson. 1970. The Radical
    Suburb: Soundings in Changing American Character.
    Philadelphia: Westminster Press.

Palmer, S. 1976. "Shakti: The Spiritual Science of DNA."
    Unpublished Master's thesis, Concordia University,
    Montreal.

Prince, R. 1975. "Cocoon Work." In Religious Movements in
    Contemporary America. I. Zaretsky and M. Leone (eds.).
    Princeton, N. J.: Princeton University Press: 255-274.

Rosen, P. 1976. "Psychobabble." New Times (November): 49-
    58.

Rozak, T. 1969. Making of a Counterculture. New York:
    Doubleday.

Sennett, R. 1974. The Fall of Public Man. Cambridge:
    Cambridge University Press.

Slater, P. 1970. The Pursuit of Loneliness. Boston: Beacon
    Press.

Smith, A. 1975. Powers of the Mind. New York: Ballantine
    Books.

Stone, D. 1976. "The Human Potential Movement." In C. Glock
    and R. Bellah, eds. The New Religious Consciousness.
    Berkeley: University of California Press: 93-115.

Tipton, Steve. 1977. "est and Ethics: Rule-Egoism in Middle
    Class Culture." Paper presented at the annual convention
    of the American Psychological Association, September.

Tiryakian, E. A. (ed.). 1974. On the Margin of the Visible.
    New York: John Wiley and Sons.

Tobey, A. 1976. "The Summer Solstice of the Healthy-Happy-
    Holy Organization." In C. Glock and R. Bellah (eds.).
    The New Religious Consciousness. Berkeley: University
    of California Press: 5-30.

Troeltsch, Ernst. 1931. Social Teaching of the Christian Churches. New York: The MacMillan Co. Pub.

Turner, R. 1976. "The Real Self: From Institution to Impulse." American Journal of Sociology, 81, No. 5: 989-1016.

Wallis, R. 1977. The Road to Total Freedom: A Sociological Analysis of Scientology. New York: Columbia University Press.

Weber, M. 1925. Economy and Society. New York: Bedminster Press, 1968.

_____. 1958. The Religion of India. New York: Free Press.

Weigart and Hastings. 1977. "Identity Loss, Family and Social Change." AJS, Vol. 82, No. 6: 1171-85.

Westley, F. 1977. "Searching For Surrender." American Behavioral Scientist, 20, 6: 925-40.

Whitehead, H. 1976. "Reasonably Fantastic: Some Perspectives on Science Fiction, Scientology and the Occult." In Religious Movements in Contemporary America. I. Zaretsky and M. Leone (eds.). Princeton, N. J.: Princeton University Press: 547-90.

Wilson, B. 1976. Contemporary Transformations of Religion. New York: Oxford University Press.

Wuthnow, R. 1976a. "The New Religions in a Social Context." In C. Glock and R. Bellah (eds.), The New Religious Consciousness. University of California Press: 267-294.

_____. 1976b. The Consciousness Reformation. Berkeley: University of California Press.

Yai-fai Ho, David. 1976. "On the Concept of Face." AJS, Vol. 81, #4: 867-884.

Yinger, M. I. 1957. Religion, Society and the Individual. New York: The Macmillan Co.

Zaretsky, I. and M. P. Leone. 1975. Religious Movements in Contemporary America. Princeton, N. J.: Princeton University Press.

Zaretsky, I. I. 1975. "In the Beginning was the Word." In Religious Movements in Contemporary America. I. I. Zaretsky and M. P. Leone (eds.). Princeton: Princeton University Press: 166-222.

APPENDIX

Research tools: Interview schedule and
group survey index form

CONCORDIA UNIVERSITY

INTERVIEW SCHEDULE

Contemporary Self-Development Groups

(November 1974)

1. What are the <u>names</u> (is the name) of the new religious, para-religious, or human growth groups with which you are currently involved?

   (List here the one or two groups with which the subject is primarily involved. Other such groups may be listed under 7a. In relation to the questions about the aims and techniques, answer with regard to the group from whom we received the name of subject, indicating as well goals and techniques associated with other groups).

2. <u>How long</u> have you been involved as a regular participant?

3. How would you <u>describe</u> your <u>present</u> <u>involvement</u> with this group?

3a Do you participate in any kind of <u>group meetings</u>? (Indicate interval, kind of meeting-retreat, exercise class, etc.).

4. Do you hold any kind of <u>leadership</u> positions?

   If so, how long:
   If so, how were you chosen (and trained, if necessary)
   Any prior positions?

5. Any <u>others</u> of your immediate family also involved? If yes, how many?

5a How does your family feel about your involvement in this group?

5b Of your 5 closest friends right now, how many involved in this group?

6. <u>How did you get involved with this group</u>? What events or factors led up to your involvement?

   a) How did you <u>first</u> come in <u>contact</u> with the group?

   b) Had <u>you heard</u> of the group prior to this time?

   c) If so, what kinds of things have you heard?

   d) Did you <u>know anyone</u> in the <u>group</u> or who had been in the group? How many?

e) Initially, what did you find
especially attractive about the
group?

Its ideas

Its practices

The people involved

The claimed results

Its leaders

Other things

f) Did you at first have any doubt
about becoming involved?

g) Did anyone try to dissuade you
from becoming involved? Who?
Why?

7. Before and since becoming involved with this group had you
ever been involved with any other similar groups? What
other groups and in what sequence were you involved?
Explain.

8. Personally, what do you hope to realize as a result of
your involvement with this group or with these groups?
(To interviewer: just list specific goals associated
with participation in this group or with these groups;
those listed in question one; note any aims listed
below as mentioned by subject).

8a Have your goals changed since becoming involved in this
group? If so, how?

8b On these cards are listed some of the ways in which people
have described their aims for participating in these kinds
of groups. Do any of these correspond to your own goals?
Which of these aims have greater priority for you? How
successful have you been in achieving these aims?

1) To be able to enjoy my life
more of the time

2) To achieve psychic
detachment

3) To realize the experience
of community

4) To help usher in an age of
peace

5) To revitalize my spiritually
or religious life

    6) To develop <u>spiritual</u> and/or
       <u>psychic</u> <u>powers</u>

    7) To realize some kind of
       special peak experience

    8) To become an integrated,
       whole person

    9) To develop a <u>higher</u> <u>state</u>
       of <u>consciousness</u>

9. Do you practice any special disciplines, rituals or
techniques in hopes of realizing these goals?

    1) <u>Breathing</u> <u>exercises</u>

    2) <u>Postures</u>

    3) <u>Adherence</u> <u>to</u> <u>certain</u> <u>moral</u>
       <u>principles</u>

    4) <u>Concentration</u> <u>of</u> <u>mind</u> <u>on</u>
       <u>objects</u> <u>and</u> <u>thoughts</u>

    5) <u>Encounter</u> <u>group</u> <u>sessions</u>

    6) Exercises using <u>rhythmic</u> <u>or</u>
       <u>stylized</u> <u>body</u> <u>motions</u>

    7) Diet

    8) Meditation

    9) Chanting/singing

    10) Self-awareness exercises

    11) Hearing the experiences of
        others

    12) Service to others

    13) Prayer

    14) Worship/ritual

    15) Other

9a How often do you do each of these rituals/techniques?

9b What is your basis for feeling these techniques, rituals
and/or disciplines that will enable you to achieve the
goals you named?

    1) Have you or anyone you know had
       <u>experiential</u> <u>validation</u> of these
       techniques?

2) Has there been any kind of
   empirical or scientific
   verification of efficacy
   of these techniques?

3) Philosophically, how would
   you justify the use of these
   techniques?

4) Belief statement.

10. Have you ever experienced anything that you might
    describe as an altered state of consciousness?

10a Have you ever had any experiences which you think are an
    example of extra sensory perception? Explain.

11. Has your involvement with this group or activity led you
    to change any life patterns or habits?

    (Probes)

    1) For example, what you eat and drink

    2) Or, for example, smoking/use of
       drugs

    3) Your relations with job or work?
       Relations with parents, family.

    4) Your relations with your friends

    5) Sexual relations

    6) Any of your emotions

    7) Your recreational activities

    8) Reading, thinking

    9) Your sleep

    10) Attitudes towards money

12. General Background Information:

    Now we would like to ask you some questions about your
    present life circumstances.

    A. Sex:

    B. What year were you born in

        Where were you born

        (If alien, ask when they arrived
        in Quebec and Canada)

C. What is your present <u>marital status</u>?
(Interviewer may record this information below)

How long has this been your status?

How many children have you?

Age of oldest child

Age of youngest child

D. What is your occupation?
(Ask for the name or type of work defined in occupational terms rather than for the name of the company, etc.)

Are you working full or part time?

How long have you been employed at this job?

In what category did your yearly income for 1973 fall? (n.b. hand the Subject the card with income groups)

E. What are the last three regular jobs you have held? Most recent first.

F. Are you attending school:
(Full time, Part time)

Have you graduated from high school?

How many years of education have you had beyond high school?

G. What were the major occupations of your parents? (Father, Mother)

How many years of education have your parents had? (Code with reference to high school graduation) (Father, Mother)

H. What kind of involvements have you had with <u>formal</u> <u>religious</u> <u>groups</u>: as a child, young person

Which religious groups was it?

Are you more or less religious
now than, say, 10 years ago? Why?

What is or was the religious
preference of your Father, Mother?

13. With what other kinds of activities, groups or organizations are you currently involved?

Probes

1. Other groups/organizations

2. Occupational

3. Civic and political

4. Social

5. Religious

6. Recreational

13a In what ways are your involvements in these other
activities related to involvement in this group?

13b Do you meet with or see other members of this group in
these other activities outside your formal participation
in the group? If yes, how many?

14. Overall, how important is your involvement in this
group(s) to your present way of life? Does it somehow
lie behind your whole approach to life?

15. What do you consider were the major events of your life
during the past ten or fifteen years?

1. Family relations

2. Personal relations

3. Occupation

4. Education

5. Values

6. Religion

7. Well Being

8. Others

9. Were there periods in the past when
you can recall feeling especially
happy or at peace with the world?
(Note times and occasions)

10. Were you involved in any kinds of social or political action groups? Times and comments.

11. At what age did you leave home?

12. Could you describe the kinds of living arrangements you have been in since you left home?

16. Could you describe in a general way the characteristics of the family in which you grew up?

   (a) Was there any divorce (1), separation (2), major parental conflicts (3) or not (4)?

   (b) Did your family enjoy certain common activities together: such as holidays, recreational activities, religious activities, work activities?

   (c) Did you often (2), sometimes (1), never (3), talk over your feelings, activities, ideas with your father (4), mother (5), or both (6)?

   (d) Do you still keep close contact with your mother/father (if alive) and with your brothers/sisters (if relevant)?

   (e) Did your family have any relatively regular contact with relatives? Did your family friends with whom they sometimes/often did things?

   (f) How were important decisions made? no pattern (1), consensus (2) discussion and collective agreements (3), discussion but individual decisions (4), decisions usually made by one parent with other parent agreeing (5) decisions made by one parent?

   (g) How were you punished as a child? How was it decided that you needed to be punished? How did you feel about these punishments?

   (h) Was your family run by strict rules? How did you feel about that?

   (i) As a child did you have some specific family responsibilities? such as? How were these determined? How did/do you feel about these?

17. What was your life situation like immediately prior to your becoming involved with this group? Was it any different than it is today?

   1. At that time or shortly thereafter were there any changes in your residency? If so, what kind?

   2. Family and/or personal relations; If so, what kind?

   3. In your careers in employment and/or education. If so, what kind?

   4. How were you feeling at this time?

   5. Clear sense of life's meaning/ little or no sense of life's meaning?

   6. How long had you felt this way?

   7. Had you been actively seeking to deal with the kinds of problems bothering you/interesting you?

18. What do you consider to be your primary goals or purpose in life?

19. On these cards are listed some ways in which people have identified their life goals. Do any of these listed life-goals correspond to your own? Which do you feel are more important than others?

   1. To achieve success in my career

   2. To find satisfaction in my work

   3. To find satisfaction in my personal and family relationships

   4. To become an integrated person

   5. To help create a more peaceful, and a more just world

   6. To serve God

   7. To realize spiritual enlightenment

   8. To live in tune with nature

   9. To enjoy myself

   10. To help others fulfill themselves

   11. To reach a higher state of consciousness

          12. Other

20. Why is there so much suffering in the world?

    1. Caused by social arrangements

    2. People are just naturally
       selfish

    3. The work of the devil

    4. People don't obey God

    5. Being punished for what they did
       in a previous life

    6. Usually bring suffering on them-
       selves

    7. They haven't learned how to find
       inner peace

    8. Because science has not found out
       yet what causes suffering

    9. Just because there is

21. What do you feel are the major problems facing human
kind today? Why?

    1. Facing people in Canada?

    2. People in Quebec?

    3. You and your friends?

22. Do you feel that individuals can have any measurable
influence on government or on the economy or even on
the major events of one's own life? Why?

23. Could you describe your beliefs about life after death?

23a Is what people do and think during their life related to
the possible conditions of life after death?

24. What does the word "God" mean to you?

25. What kinds of factors do you now think have the greatest
influence on your life?

    1. Luck

    2. Upbringing

    3. Changing needs and interests
       of the world around?

    4. Will power?

    5. Spiritual insights?

6. What people in power decide?

7. Friends and loved ones?

8. God or some supernatural force?

9. Endowment

26. (To Interviewer): What are your overall impressions of

(a) the interviewer?

(b) the subject?

CONCORDIA UNIVERSITY

Survey of Contemporary Self-Development Groups

Index Form (Revised September 1974)

1. <u>Organizational Data</u>:

 1. Name and Address:

   a. Name of Association

   b. Address in Montreal

   c. Telephone Number

   d. Local leader(s)

   e. Contact person: (Name and relation to group)
      Indicate other sources of information

   f. Address of other facilities used in Montreal or
      any rural retreats

 2. Relation of local association to larger movement:

   a. How many other groups of this movement are in
      Quebec? Canada?

   b. How many other groups of this movement are in
      North America?

   c. Where is the Canadian or North American centre
      for this movement?

   d. Does the parent organization do any of the
      following:

     (i) train and/or select local leaders?

     (ii) collect dues from the local group?

     (iii) keep records of local membership?

     (iv) initiate local members?

     (v) finance local activities?

     (vi) supply local group with audio-visual media?

     (vii) supply local group with printed media?

     (viii) no parent organization

   e. Does the parent organization have any affiliated
      sub-divisions?

3. History of the Association:

    a. What is the local history of the group? (Be sure to include previous addresses which the group had in the Montreal area, as well as names of the original founding members)

    b. What role did the parent organization have in establishing the local centre?

    c. What do you know about the international history of this association?

4. Physical Setting of the Local Centre:

    a. Describe the physical setting of the local centre. Be sure to include the following: Rooms for devotion? Distinctive architecture? Printing facilities? Office facilities? Living quarters?

    b. Symbols and photographs displayed?

    c. Is the centre owned or rented? At what cost?

5. Basis of Economic Support:

    a. How is the movement supported locally?

        By donations

        Sales of crafts, food, literature

        employment of core members

        fees for instructions

6. Participation:

    a. What is the total number of local adherents (approximately)?

    b. How many people were in the group?

        one year ago?

        two years ago?

        three years ago?

    c. How many of the local adherents speak French? (percentage), English? Other? (Specify)

    d. Has the composition of the group with regard to language background of members changed over the past year or two? Explain:

    e. How many of the local adherents are of what age? (By percentage):

    f. Has the composition of the group with regard to age of members changed over the past year or two? Explain.

    g. Are there formal categories for membership?

7. Core Members and Leadership: (core adherents defined thusly: full time participants and/or assuming leadership responsibility for training or giving lessons to persons other and persons who see themselves as specifically qualified on the basis of training, experience and accomplishments):

    a. How many core members?

        Nos. of these Francophones

        Nos. of these women

    b. How is the core membership chosen?

    c. Do the core members live together at the local centre?

    d. What are the responsibilities of the core members? (i.e. division of labour among leaders)

    e. What financial arrangements do core members have with the local centre?

    f. What relationship do the core members have with the general membership?

    g. How many core members became core members before coming to the Montreal area?

    h. Do core or regular members wear any distinctive dress?

    i. How are decisions made regarding policy and activities of group?

8. Publicity:

What kinds of things is group doing to recruit new members?

        printed material?

        TV ads?

        newspaper ads?

        word of mouth?

        other?

II Techniques & Rituals

9. Which of the following are practiced by adherents either
   alone or with others? Indicate the frequency of these
   practices and whether they are primarily practiced
   collectively, privately, or both.

   1. Adherence to moral codes
   2. Chanting
   3. Devotion of leader
   4. Sacramental meal
   5. Collective songs
   6. Prayers
   7. Speaking in tongues
   8. Hatha Yoga
   9. Breathing exercises
   10. Physical exercises
   11. Hallucinatory drugs
   12. Dance
   13. Use of mantras
   14. Testimonials
   15. Silent meditation
   16. Story telling
   17. Rhythm
   18. Massage
   19. Dieting
   20. Martial arts
   21. Role playing
   22. Encounter groups
   23. Dream fantasy
   24. Concentration
   25. Sacred readings
   26. Meditation on Mandala
   27. Darshan
   28. Work
   29. Devotion
   30. Other
   (Indicate 4 most emphasized activities)

10. Consider the threefold typology of meditation techniques
    suggested by C. Naranjo and R. Ornstein in On the
    Psychology of Meditation:

     i) <u>Concentrative or absorptive meditation</u> which employs externally given symbols such as holy diagrams (YANTRAS) or verbal formulas (MANTRAS)

    ii) The <u>way of self-expression</u> in which the individual dwells upon material deriving from his own inner fantasy, and,

   iii) The <u>negative way</u> in which the meditator puts his efforts into moving away from all objects and avoiding identification with anything he can conceive of.

Do the meditation techniques taught by this particular group correspond to any of these three categories?

11. Rationale for techniques and practices:

What kinds of rationale and justification does the group offer for encouraging the particular practices which they emphasize?

(a) Do they use some kind of philosophical or metaphysical or theological rationale? Explain.

(b) Do they variously try to explain what factors within the self or in terms of the self's relation to a deity, make these practices effective? (i.e. Do they have a philosophical anthropology?) (If a and b overlap, answer them together).

(c) To what extent do they justify these practices by appealing to the experiential validation of members? What kinds of validating experiences do they point to?

(d) Do they justify the use of these practices by appealing to external or scientific verification? If yes, then what kinds of evidence do they find to be persuasive? Explain.

12. Could you describe the steps through which new members proceed on their way to becoming more active, more skilled adherents and finally to achieving the highest goals of the group?

(a) To what extent does there seem to be an orderly progression in the training or development of adherents?

(b) What kinds of things are required to be initiates? Is there a class for initiates? What things are required of newly initiated members?

(c) Are there intermediate courses or disciplines which more active or trained adherents seek to master? Is it fairly easy or difficult to pass through these intermediate stages? Describe.

(d) What kinds of language do adherents use to describe
the final stage of personal development? How easy
or difficult is it to achieve this goal? Explain.

13. Do members of this association seek to achieve or
experience higher or altered states of consciousness?
If they do, what kinds of language do they use to
describe these experiences? From their perspective,
what are the signs of these kinds of experiences? Do
they consider such experiences to be the primary goal
of involvement in these associations or an accompaniment
of other goals? Describe.

14. Which of the following traditional religious rituals are
established and regularly performed by this group?

1. Birth celebrations

2. Puberty rites

3. Marriage ceremonies

4. Funeral rites

5. Memorial festivals for important historic dates,
like Passover, Easter, birth of Buddha

6. New Years festivals

7. Spring festivals

8. Weekly collective devotion

9. Comments:

14a Are any of these "traditional" religious rituals
celebrated "non-traditionally?"

15. Over the course of a week, typically what kinds of
involvements would adherents have with this association
and its practices? In addition to private rituals, what
collective gatherings would adherents participate in or
in addition to the collective activities, what kinds of
private meditation or exercises would individuals
practice? Describe (if not already covered above).

III Beliefs and Goals:

16. Goals of the Association:

Are the aims of this association primarily defined in
relation to worldly, secular values or specially defined
religious ends? In answering this question, answer these
sub-questions:

(a) What terms does this association use to describe the
goals and values it seeks to realize?

(b) Which of the following goals do they consider to be
important or not important; for their adherent:

to achieve integration or centered-
ness of self

to achieve self-control

to achieve greater health

to develop psychic powers

to achieve an ecstatic, trance-
like vision

to achieve an ecstatic, still-
pointed mind

devotion to master

God-realization

other

(c) Does the association view itself as being religious?
(If not religious, then what kinds of groups or
activities would they consider to be religious?).
If yes, on what basis?

(d) Does the association view itself as being a new
science or a new para-science or a new therapy?
Explain.

17. Ideas About Present and Future:

Are there millenarian or apocalyptic elements in the
belief system of this group? Do they believe in the
end of the age? heralded by extraordinary events or
persons?

18. Ideas About Salvation:

Since these groups are all seeking to bring some kind of
special benefit to help persons overcome their present
distresses, how do these associations describe both the
present predicaments which must be overcome and the
basis for hoping that the practices of this group will
help persons to transform themselves so as to overcome
these predicaments?

(a) What are the predicaments that must be overcome?
(In the language of the group?)

(b) What is the basis (described in the language of the
association) or ground or source of power for the
transformation of self which the group proclaims as
a possibility?

19. World View:

To what extent does this association have its own world
view that contrasts with the dominant world view and

value orientation of Canadian society (i.e. with the
ideals of individual self-development through work and
achievements), etc.

DATE DUE	BORROWER'S NAME
DEC 29	DIXON, BARB 348710
	PO BOX 1791 LAW, KS 66044
	SA
MAY 16 2001	SA renew
	notice 7/26